Passive Inco

Discover the top 5 new ideas to make money in 2020. From zero to financial freedom with your skills and passions. The complete guide with tips, pros & cons for each business

Martin Wilder

Table of Contents

By the same author:

This is a perfect guide if you are looking for a new way to build your financial freedom, working from home or wherever you want. All the secrets to creating a profitable business online, and all the tips to avoid mistakes that will make you waste time and money

Introduction

The mode of communication between businesses and other businesses as well as their customers has radically changed over the years—from messengers, letters, fax machines, telephones and now, the Internet, which is the fastest mode of communication yet. This gives online businesses an added advantage on their path to success. The amount of business that is being conducted online as well as the number of people using the Internet is growing at an extremely high rate. With a growing number of internet-enabled devices and the ever-increasing affordability and availability of Internet access makes the online spectrum to be a very lucrative business to conduct business. The world currently has well over 1 billion Internet users, most of whom are web savvy and tech-savvy. Among the most common Internet usage trends among these users are study, research, socializing, and also doing some online shopping.

This in itself answers the question as to why a large majority of businesses are taking their business online at such a high rate. Your business is open to many amazing opportunities when you have it online. Apart from the large market that is available on the Internet, the cost of carrying out business online is significantly lower as compared to having and running a traditional offline business. There are a lot of overhead costs that are not incurred while running an online business. Some of these costs include warehousing costs, premise leasing costs, high staff salaries, and other inherent costs incurred by offline businesses.

A majority of offline businesses that transferred part or all of their business online are experiencing the advantages of conducting their operations online. They are continually investing more and more resources to make sure that their online business stays ahead of the pack.

It is undeniable that the Internet will eventually make its way into all aspects of personal and business communications. A few years ago, having an Internet connection at work or at home was more of a trend or a luxury, but having an active internet connection is quickly becoming a norm, and in some cases, a necessity.

As new online security-based technologies are being developed every other day, the general understanding and trust in online transactions are on the rise. Groups that provide information about buying and making money are coming up every day in the blogosphere and also in social media platforms. These groups help educate the masses regarding those topics and make people more comfortable with an online business.

The amazing thing about the Internet, it is an amazing place to start earning some passive income on the side without spending so much time and resources. Online business is not restricted to just selling products and offering your services; there are many more avenues you can make money some of which are so automated that you only have to do some marketing and watch your money grow.

In this book, we will have an in-depth look at some of these avenues and help you get some insight and make an informed decision as to the model that works well with you.

Chapter 1: Starting a Business

Everybody wants to start a business and be their own boss, or maybe just to generate a little income on the side. Many people do actualize this dream, some become very successful, and others fail. The main motivating factors that push people to start businesses of their own are:

- Desire to be self-employed
- The desire to achieve a certain social status
- Ability to enjoy their freedom of creativity
- Ability to implement your knowledge and skills
- Financial freedom

The Small Business Administration is of the opinion that these reasons are likely to be an advantage for some but not all people. These are the people with the right kind of mindset to ensure that their investment or project emerges on the other side of the storm in one piece. This is an entrepreneurial mindset, and we will have an in-depth look at it in this chapter.

Before we, however, dwell further into the mindset of an entrepreneur, let us have a look at the common fears that people have and prevent them from starting their own alternative streams of earning passive income.

- **Money**: You can't get very far without money. What to do: line up original funding early enough or at least enough study has been undertaken to have a strategy to raise cash.
- **Security**: Many people don't want to sacrifice the constant revenue of nine-to-five jobs. What to do: don't offer up the work that provides the current source of income. Connect with someone or operate the company part-time to assist in operating your company—a "co-founder."
- **Competition**: Many individuals are unable to differentiate their company thoughts from comparable thoughts. What to do: find out how to do a cheaper, quicker, or superior thing.
- Many people simply don't understand what kind of company they want to get into. What to do: figure out good patterns. Remember a franchise. Find an answer to something that annoys you—businesspeople call it a "point of pain"—and attempt to transform it into a company.

The Mindset to Start a Business

If we look at the concept of entrepreneurship a little more carefully, we can define three features of entrepreneurship:

1) Business running: A company provides funds for the production of products or services. Entrepreneurship implies setting up a profit-making company.

2) Innovation: Entrepreneurship usually implies the introduction of a fresh item, the application of a new method or technology, the opening of a new sector, or the development of a fresh type of organization to produce or improve a commodity.

3) Risk-Taking: The word risk implies that it is impossible to know the result of the entrepreneurial undertaking. Therefore, entrepreneurs are always operating under some degree of uncertainty, and they are unable to predict the results of many of the choices they have to create. As a result, many of the measures they take are driven primarily by their trust in technology and their knowledge of the company setting in which they operate.

Difference between an Entrepreneur and a Business Owner

An entrepreneur is an innovator who conceives an idea, grows it to provide solutions that are not being adequately addressed in the market at the time. An entrepreneur aims at providing solutions where there are none so that their businesses can grow and expand to other markets.

A business owner is someone who creates a business and operates it for the sole purpose of generating some extra income. Significant growth and expansion are most of the time a priority in their list of objectives, but rather financing short term personal or family expenses. Sometimes such businesses are referred to as lifestyle businesses, and some of them include neighborhood fast-food joints.

Characteristics of an Entrepreneur

Becoming a successful business owner needs sound planning, creativity, and hard work, as well as taking hazards, as all companies need some type of investment, generally time or cash. To start assessing whether you are right to start your own business, you may want to consider looking at the common and outstanding qualities of effective entrepreneurs:

Persistence and Resilience

Businesses of persistence and resilience, like everything else, take time to develop. During the initial stages of being in business, very few individuals will generate massive quantities of profit. Even if your company is effective, there will be stuff that you fail. For a multitude of reasons, some initiatives inevitably fail—poor scheduling, rivals providing better alternatives, market timing, or other variables. You need to know and develop from your errors in order to be a good entrepreneur. You have to be prepared to live with uncertainty and conquer barriers you have not anticipated.

Innovation and Creativity

Initiating an idea or concept is the first move towards beginning a company. It requires innovation to develop a commodity—be it physical, digital, or service that is unique and is of value to consumers—product or service that brings value to customers that they cannot get elsewhere requires innovation. In addition, entrepreneurs often have to discover innovative methods to tackle everyday company issues such as early inventory shipping providers and inadequate marketing plans.

Flexibility

Even the business intentions that are most well thought out will alter along with the manner. Changes are supposed to occur in the industry, technology, and client tastes, and they are out of your control. The key to the survival of your business will be your capacity to be versatile and react to these modifications.

Passion

As you likely know, it is not simple to be entrepreneurial. If you're not enthusiastic about what you're doing, persisting through all the difficulties that come your way will be much more difficult. Also, your clients will realize, selling something you're not enthusiastic about yourself is more difficult. "You have to be passionate about it. Otherwise, it's not worth doing. Owning your own business is not easy, and it's not going to make you rich quick. You're going to be in it for the long haul, so it's got to be something you love."

To start your own business, you need to have a certain mindset. This is the mindset that separates the serious businessmen from the jokers. As you are starting your business, you need to follow the following rules and ensure that you start your path to gaining some passive income with the right footing.

1. Conduct a Self-analysis

Everyone who embarks on starting a business always feels like they are up to the task. After choosing an interest that they feel has the potential to generate some extra money on the side, many entrepreneurs believe the only thing they will need to do is to establish a business then it is downhill all the way. For those who do not have an interest that can be monetized, they often choose markets or products they can easily source or have a wide array of knowledge about. The sad reality, however, is that a large majority of people who are starting a business do not have the adequate knowledge necessary to handle starting up a business.

The beauty of learning is that it never ends at school, and therefore, you can always learn whatever you do not know. Simple. The first thing you need to do is to identify what it is you do not know what information or skill is it that you lack to make your business venture profitable. To do this, you need to ask yourself in order to realize your strengths and weaknesses.

a) Do you have the constant urge to always telling people about your success?

b) Are you disciplined enough to work without supervision and getting distracted?

c) Do you need encouragement from friends and family whenever you are engaging in a new project?

d) If you are married, do you discuss with them about your projects and how they are bound to affect your living conditions?

e) If you are planning to quit your main job to start your business, how are you going to cope with the new working environment?

f) Would you be able to cope and bounce back up if your venture fails at the first attempt?

g) Is it just a fantasy, or are you serious about starting your own business?

h) When others quit, do you follow suit or look for creative ways around the problem?

By studying these issues, you should be prepared to begin to see the kind of character that is better adapted to be an entrepreneur. For example, if you're someone who loves to be part of a team, share anecdotes, and chat on a Monday morning over the water or coffee machine, then the loneliness that always comes when you're working for yourself won't be for you. Don't work under the false assumption that everything will be alright on the night. That's never the situation. In reality, what can go wrong will generally go wrong, along with a number of other unforeseen issues.

2. Develop Self-reliance

I encountered loads of promising entrepreneurs by beginning and operating my own companies, who overcame all kinds of difficulties to begin their own effective companies. What they all have, without exception, is an intense feeling of self-reliance. They fully believe that whatever life or business may throw at them, they have the power to overcome, whatever it may be.

They also completely acknowledge that they are accountable for their own future on their own. This is crucial to their achievement—the unshakeable conviction that they are responsible for their lives, and they alone. Yes, their companies are resulted by occurrences that are often beyond their command. But by accepting that success is not dependent on what happens to you, but how you react to these events, you will begin to realize that ultimately your success depends on no one but you.

3. Have Written Goals

You undertake to achieve whatever you want when you set a stated objective, which could be anything from just spending half an hour a day investigating your fresh company to set a starting point for your fresh company.

Just believe how motivating it is to write down the date you plan to begin your business. Imagine the forces beginning to work on a conscious and unconscious stage for a time, pushing you toward this objective. Once you have a start date in mind, you can follow it up with the following:

- Note down all the achievements you want to have made by the time you get to your set date.
- Refine this list to smaller, more achievable goals.
- For these items, create a written schedule. There's no point in saying that by such a date you're going to get them done. In order to accomplish your objectives, you need to operate on a schedule.
- Review your original date if needed. You may not have provided yourself a reasonable timeframe in which to operate. This is a prevalent error created by novice entrepreneurs who will underestimate how long it takes for financing to be put in place, provider contracts, and so on.

As you can see, you'll go from merely thinking or dreaming about doing something to genuinely work towards a fixed, written objective when you set written objectives. And this will significantly improve your potential likelihood of achievement.

4. Develop a "Can-Do" Attitude

Like creating a true feeling of dependence, effective entrepreneurs have a true' can - do' approach as well. You understand what kind of individual I mean. You'll discover them running local community campaigns, addressing issues head-on, and unwilling to accept' no' for anybody's response. When you've been on vacation, you'll have encountered these individuals. They are the people who get it settled rapidly without fuss or insult when there is an issue.

Unlike others, with an unshakeable faith in their skills, can-doers live their lives. They refuse to be told (regardless of the circumstance) that anything they are about to do is impossible. Imagine for a time how it must have been the first individuals to take an aircraft across the Atlantic for the Wright brothers. Picture if you're going to argue and forecast all those from the' it-cannot-be-done' camp.

Lesser people would not have been disturbed by such a task, and some would have said they were dumb and careless. But their accomplishment brought appreciation globally and at the moment, led to the fact that ordinary people could quickly travel from America to Europe by plane.

For your potential achievement as a self-employed business person, a "can-do" approach is essential. If you are only able to accomplish outcomes where the odds are placed in your favor, and achievement is assured, you might remain to do whatever you do now because the only thing between you and failure will be your stance at moments on the path ahead. It's not what's happening to you in this lifetime, but how you're responding to it.

Start working immediately to become a "can-do." Guard against listening to people's floods that tell you anything you're about to do won't work. Believe in yourself and work to remove personal doubts and fears.

5. Keep Your Own Counsel

If you're the sort of individual you've got to say all of your upcoming company plans, then save yourself from potential agonies and decide not to begin your own company now. It's really devastating to share your intentions with everyone else. You will be bombarded with free, well-meaning, and completely pointless tips as quickly as you choose to inform someone you're thinking about beginning your own company. So, hold your thoughts for yourself with the strongest will.

From when you start your own company, the only individuals you should ever debate or give tips are those who are already managing good companies. There's nobody else. If this idea still has an issue, let me ask you a query. Have you ever been to a group where you encountered a specialist like a physician, architect, technician, dentist, or the like who requested you for guidance on how to handle their clients, layout their houses or build their devices? Naturally not. And for businessmen, the same is true. Nobody but you is really skilled in knowing what is required in beginning your company, let alone sufficiently skilled to provide guidance.

Simply remember always to be your own counsel.

What You Need to Do

Choose the Right Niche

The mistake many people make when they are trying to sell a product is making the product and then researching a market for it. The reverse should be the case whereby you research for a niche market that does a lot of spending then developing the product that best suits the needs of that market.

This, however, is easier said than done, but there are numerous places on the Internet where you can conduct your market research for free. This is because these websites have done all the research for you, and you just need to find the right information source to make your work easier.

While doing your research, you will come across many niche markets where you think you can make a killing of butt there are a couple of important factors you need to figure out in order to determine how well you and your business are bound to perform if you chose to venture into that market.

    a) Whether you have a passion for the niche, if not, whether or not you will be able to develop a passion for the niche that will last in the long term.

b) Whether other people have a passion for that particular niche and if they have a pressing issue, they need to be solved.

c) The size of the market is important because if it is not so big, it may be difficult for your business to have a smooth start due to too much competition.

d) How well do people spend in this niche market?

e) What other similar products are selling well in this niche? Can you give a more superior product or a different product all together that is lacking in this niche?

f) At what prices are these products being sold for in the niche market? Will your business make a profit by selling at similar prices? Is your competition selling the products at a lower price so that they can generate revenue on the back-end, cross-selling or are they upselling?

- **Back-end Sales** refer to a process where merchants sell a product to a customer at a low price and later on the market to the customer a more expensive product the supplier thinks might interest the customer. Normally, nut not in all cases, it is a product that complements the first product purchased.
- **Upsell** refers to when a supplier tries to sell the customer an upgraded version of the product purchased by the customer right before the

customer checks out. For example, when you are trying to buy a basic subscription from a service provider, just before the client checks out, the provider's system will ask the customer to buy the premium subscription that has better services and also a higher price tag.

- **Cross-selling** is similar to upselling, but the supplier attempts to make the client purchase complementary items. For example, if you buy a swimming costume, the supplier will also try to make you buy another swimming-related product like swimming goggles.

How to Research for Your Niche Market

For a start, it is always advisable to be in touch with what's trending and also the latest news and events of the current world. Reading newspapers, niche magazines, watching and listening to the news is a good place to start. Always have a pen and paper with you so that you can note down an idea that you think can generate some revenue.

However, we are living in a fast-moving world where new information is getting generated on the go so it would be wise to conduct your research on the Internet. Your notebook and pen should still be kept in handy, though! In this section, we will have a look at the available resources where you can carry out a free, effective, and credible niche market research.

- **Analyze Things Around You**

Simply look around your current surroundings is this technique. It might look around your home, garden, park, local stores, or whenever you're out in a fresh location. For example, you may see an internet modem and decide to teach parents about the dangers that their children may be exposed to on the Internet.

Write it down in your notebook once you discover a fresh niche concept and then proceed to look. How pointless you believe the concept will be is not important; write it down! It may well be the most lucrative of all your thoughts for the niche. Repeat the method throughout the remainder of your building, then go to your garden. However, this technique does not need to be restricted to your building. In your local park, local stores, or wherever you are, you can repeat the same method. Each location is distinct, and you will get one or more niche thoughts from each location.

- **Analyze Your Hobbies**

This is an outstanding way to generate fresh niche thoughts because if you generate a product from a niche concept that you created using this technique, you will build a company that will talk about what you enjoy to do. For this technique, all you have to do is lie down and believe for a while about what you enjoy to do, what topics you like to speak about or read about, or even what topics you know about.

Sit down and believe about everything you like to do for five or ten minutes. You should have at least 20 ideas to come up with. Write down all of them. Think about how you can transform that into a commodity once you have brainstormed your 20 hobbies and interests.

- **Analyze the Passions and Hobbies of your Social Networks**

This is comparable to the technique you used to create fresh niche thoughts using your hobbies and passions, except this technique includes using the interests of your buddies and family. If you're fortunate, with obscure interests and passions, you'll have a few friends or family members. In this manner, you can find niches that are known to very few others and dominate this micro-niche industry. A micro-niche industry, compared to other economies, is very tiny. A micro-niche industry is much simpler to dominate than a wider niche, and clients are often more enthusiastic and ready to purchase.

- **The Media**

The media have recently had an ever-increasing impact on our life and can be used as an outstanding instrument to generate fresh niche thoughts. Finding what's on-demand using media includes studying television advertisements and programs, magazine advertisements, content, and magazines. You can rapidly spot possibly profitable niche markets by evaluating current affairs. Global warming and its impacts have been publicized extensively over the past few years and increasing numbers of individuals are attempting to do their part to assist in decreasing the impacts. You could readily investigate how to decrease global warming, save cash in the process, compile it into a novel, and sell it for a bunch of cash.

Using the content of magazines is also a great way to select niche thoughts. You always see women's magazines with fashion advice and tips on weight loss (not that I read women's magazines anyway). You could use these papers as studies, and the data is clearly in demand because they are included in these journals. But don't just look at women's magazines:

1. Vehicle magazines – You could write a book about selecting the ideal vehicle to fit the customer's goals.
2. Garden Magazines – Create a book to grow a certain crop sort of a book to create a lovely garden.
3. Travel magazines – Create a travel info item for inexpensive, luxurious locations or vacation-related stuff to do.

There are thousands of journals out there, and you can get 3 or 4 fresh niche thoughts from each one. Visit www.magazines.com to browse a wide variety of types of magazines.

It is also an outstanding way to select a profitable niche market to monitor the TV listings and analyze what's on TV. If you had found that popular TV show "LOST" would have been so effective with so many fanatical viewers who are very enthusiastic about the program, an outstanding illustration of this sort of niche choice. You could have developed quite readily a "Lost Theories" book that you donate free of charge and benefit from on the back-end.

- **Using Online Tools**

Niche's choice of Internet tools mainly includes finding out what individuals are looking for and what data online they are attempting to discover out. Using the eBay pulse is one way to find out what's warm right now. The eBay pulse defines which keywords were most frequently found on the eBay search engine, and it's a great tool to identify what's warm on eBay and online.

Another way to generate fresh niche thoughts internet is to use some of Google's free keyword research instruments. First being: http:/www.google.com/trends Type Google Trends in a keyword, and it will show a graph illustrating how the number of requests has altered from 2003 to the current day. It's a great way to identify up-and-down niche economies that are declining. It also demonstrates to you what media incidents affect the significant search volumes rise or reduces. You can then recognize how this niche will be affected by press speculation. Another excellent instrument to identify niches within niches is Google Suggest (http:/labs.google.com). All you have to do for this one is typing a keyword, and with extremely sought words and sentences, Google will immediately provide you with a list of other keyword opportunities. This is a great way to reduce your view and recognize in niches (micro-niches) very warm and profitable niches.

- **Using Keyword Searches**

The number of requests per month is the most significant thing we are looking for here. One thing you should keep in mind is that the first connection only takes into account Yahoo! search engine requests, which I think is about 30 percent of complete searches per month. The main way to profit from this company is to create your own data item that will solve an issue and help the client with something they struggle with. Type keywords and sentences into your favorite keyword research instrument is an outstanding way to figure out these issues.

Benefits of Owning a Business

In-charge of Your Earnings

Working for someone else means they decide how much you will earn on a monthly basis when that amount increases and the increased rate. Your employer will also dictate the number of hours that you work, and therefore you have even lower chances of earning some extra money on the side. With your own business, you have a greater degree of control when it comes to your income. You have the freedom to set your own wage rates, and your level of income is determined by the effort you put into your business.

You Are in Control of Your Work-Life Balance

This is a major need among many employed people. If you need a personal day form the office when you are employed, you will have to ask for permission, and it is in no way guaranteed that your request will be granted. In some extreme cases, people have to beg or refuse to go to work all together and face the consequences of their actions later.

When you are running your own business, on the other hand, you have the flexibility of choosing whether or not you will go to work, or where you will conduct your business from and set your own hours.

For many entrepreneurs, having their own businesses has helped them in setting their priorities straight, and they are able to fulfill the most important responsibilities and successfully manage and grow their business.

You Can Choose Your Colleagues

While working for someone else, you will basically work with anyone, your employer supervisor or human resource instructs you to. Whether you have good relations with this person or not is most of the time not important, but getting the job done is most of the time, the number one priority. When you are running your own business, you have the freedom to set your office culture so that you can only work with people of certain qualities. You are also in most cases in charge of hiring and you, therefore, have a very strong influence when it comes to the people you work with.

The Higher the Risk, the Higher the Return

Owning a business is a risky thing. It takes a strong-willed person to invest their savings in a venture that may or may not succeed. But, as the investment saying goes, the higher the risk, the higher the return. As a business owner, you should be good at managing risks so as to reap better returns. There are very many risks and uncertain situations that affect many aspects of a company, but it is always reassuring that when you get your business operations under control, things definitely change for the better.

Just like in sports, the more you play, the better you become. Similarly, in the business arena, the more you do business, the easier it becomes for you to identify opportunities or danger when they are miles away. You are also able to create workarounds on the fly when dealing with bad situations and also get the most out of the good ones.

You Can Outdo Yourself

As other people achieve to be the best at the routine that they follow every single day. As an entrepreneur, you are busy trying to become a better version of yourself. Each day is full of new challenges and opportunities for you to grab hold of and eventually make the best out of.

Follow Your Passion

The funny reality about owning a business is that you will find yourself spending many hours a day working than you did when working for someone else. The even funnier reality is that many entrepreneurs rarely notice it because they are loving what they are doing and having fun while doing it.

Things Get Done Faster

There are peculiar characteristics of entrepreneurs of wanting things to be done faster than they currently are being done. They are mostly proactive and get things done faster. As we have seen in the previous point, entrepreneurs who do what they love have fun doing it. So, it is only natural for them to be aggressive and find ways of doing it faster and better. As the big players in the industry are feeling secure in their comfort zones, the small entrepreneurs are busy being proactive in getting more improved products for their respective niches and giving better quality services, and this translates to increased revenue and better profits.

Take Pride in Your Success

One of the major advantages of being an entrepreneur and owning your own business over being someone else's employee is the sense of pride you get in building a successful empire. There is always great joy and pride in that feeling of self-actualization.

Chapter 2: Affiliate Marketing

Over the past century, affiliate marketing has caught the imagination and attention of a variety of entrepreneurs as a continuing manner to generate revenue possibilities. Here's some history on affiliate advertising growth and how it keeps evolving today.

At its heart, affiliate marketing is about paying attention to a good or service through the use of Internet assets managed by partners or subsidiaries. The simplest of all these techniques is to allow advertising to be shown on a website which is the affiliate's domain.

Typically, the advertisement will allow the potential client to click on and redirect to a website or location where more data is available and the possibility of ordering the goods or services. The affiliate is compensated with compensation in exchange for offering a portal for that client to discover the service product, generally through electronic transition or checking.

The notion of affiliate marketing is a natural outcome of online marketing that emerged in the early years of extensive use of the Internet. Initially, online marketing was more of a business-to-business strategy, as businesses were the first to jump on the Internet bandwagon. A cost-effective way to collect fresh company customers was to set up a website and send messages to solicit from companies.

As Internet use started to spread throughout the household, a variety of businesses started to see that collaborating with holders of private websites would be an excellent way to encourage goods and services with very little investment in marketing funds.

The trick was to create the concept attractive to people, so they would be interested in allowing firms to advertise via their websites. The foundations of affiliate marketing have been created out of this need to come up with a policy that would appeal to a big number of individuals and proceed to form the course of affiliate programs today.

The vast bulk of affiliate programs, through revenue sharing, provide compensation.

Revenue sharing is sometimes referred to as a transaction cost per purchase. The affiliate essentially earns either a set quantity or a proportion of the buy cost when someone locates and purchases the product or service through the affiliate's gateway.

For example, a family website that enabled businesses that produced products for infant care to feature ads on the front page of the website, along with links, would pay the family for every sale made through that link.

Many affiliate programs involve a certain amount of income before a payout occurs. Others will pay with no minimum amount of income needed on a weekly, bi-weekly, or monthly basis.

The cost per intervention technique is another less common way to generate income through an affiliate program. This varies from the price per purchase technique by merely requiring the potential seller to view the ad on a website and tap on it to explore for a minimum quantity of moment.

In a sale, it doesn't have to stop. As one can guess, the quantity of income generated from this type of agreement is significantly lower than a scheme for distributing income per purchase.

The pay per click can be the format that most people recognize instantly with the price per action globe. It's also the least common affiliate marketing technique today, though.

While PPC started following strongly, the technique turned out to be far too prone to fraudulent clicks, resulting in little revenues but a lot of cash being paid out by advertisers.

Methods of today, which assist monitor customer accounts as well as involve a minimum quantity of browsing moments, have significantly reduced the incidence of fraud.

Today's affiliate advertising includes a wide variety of goods and services, from home to telecommunications. Any entrepreneur with some expertise in a particular region could very well discover an affiliate program that would produce some recurring revenue. A glance around the Internet is all it gets.

Common Affiliate Marketing Mistakes

While affiliate marketing is an excellent way to gain a living, many people are becoming discouraged and dropping out of programs. The inability to succeed in affiliate marketing in many cases has to do with creating a few easy errors. Here are some instances of these errors and why they should be prevented.

Perhaps the most prevalent misconception about affiliate advertising is that you can slap up a low-quality website with no original content and toss in some affiliate connections in enormous sums of income.

Although it is definitely true that in order to participate in an affiliate program, you need to have a website up and working. There is also the need to make some attempt to get the word out of your post. Otherwise, opportunities are fairly low for individuals to visit your website and click on one of the connections.

Promoting yourself and your website is a major component of ensuring affiliate income is generated. This will simply be doing all you can to increase the ranking of your search engine positions on Google, Yahoo, and MSN.

Too many individuals believe that the Internet will magically catch every beautiful term on the website somehow and magically make it prominently appear when individuals do a survey. That's not all the time. It is an absolute must to take a moment to closely investigate keywords, craft content linked to them, and optimize your location for them.

And it's not that. Marketing is greater than SEO alone. A powerful and comprehensive marketing effort involves reaching out there and using every valid means to promote your site, from placing business cards on restaurant tables to publishing a printed ad in the local supermarket to identifying your location online business and information pages.

To choose to regard this kind of exercise as a waste of moment is to decide more or less than you want the program to fail.

Another error many affiliate members create is not selecting products that are relevant to your website's material. For instance, you operate a fantastic website about dog care and coaching. People are going to visit your page to see your pets ' pictures, read your remarks on different elements of dog training, and maybe post a message or two.

Since your tourists are already interested in animals, why not create sure that the advertisements on your page have something to do with animals or animal care? If that's the situation, you'll gain a lot more cash than advertisements that have to do with home decoration or some other topic.

Maintaining your website material and advertisements more or less appropriate to each other will create income generation easier, and as an affiliate marketer, it will not fail. Now, this may seem intuitive–but many create this error in subtle respects (i.e., they disagree with goods with their customers).

One ultimate error many affiliate marketers create is not occasionally sprucing up their websites. Keeping the material new is one way to build and keep a reading crowd loyal.

If there is a reason to check home with your website every week, then it is likely that repeated visitors will tap on advertisements that appear to be fresh to them, or that they have liked looking at the last moment they visited your website.

It is a sure way to restrict your likelihood of being a good affiliate marketer to keep the same ancient look and the same old text with nothing fresh to attract people back.

In short, most of the most common errors go back to an attitude that you don't have to do anything to produce income.

The reality is, you need to encourage your site proactively, maintain the material fresh, and make sure the advertisements have some link to your site's topic matter.

You will have much better chances of being a success with affiliate marketing by having the time and energy to do these three easy stuffs.

Getting Started

While there is not much cost to start up as an affiliate marketer, if you really want to create cash selling the products of other people, there are a few things you need to do.

Here are some fundamental tips to assist you in getting everything you need to do before you sign up for the first affiliate program.

One of the fundamental requirements of any good affiliate program is to have your own website. While the website ad rooms can be purchased and advertised via Google AdWords, this is a short-term approach.

Establishing a fundamental website with a specific focus will create all the difference to your program's achievement in the world. Keep in mind that a lot of flash media, animation or other fancy bells and whistles don't have to complicate your website.

Indeed, if you're planning to focus on affiliate marketing policies that target the home customer, you're better off with a fundamental location that will rapidly load on a dial-up connection. After all, in a variety of places, dial-up is still highly common.

While you may choose to go to a free website, if you go with your own domain name, you will discover it much simpler to work with affiliate programs. Securing a domain name and room on a remote server these days is very simple and cheap. For a small monthly fee, some companies will provide you with both facilities.

They may also often have basic software to help you design and upload your pages to the server, even if you don't know the technology particularly well.

Another significant element is to determine what your contact data will be about your affiliate program communication. This would include a physical mailing address and an email address. The email address should be specific to the marketing company that you have set aside.

You may consider it useful to get a free email address, although you will definitely look more professional if the email address seems to be leading to some kind of company.

Often, when you receive a domain name, you will have the choice to have one email address. If that's the situation, follow this path and use it for any email correspondence as your touch.

Determine where you may want your affiliate checks to be mailed as far as your physical mailing address is concerned. If you're not sure why the bills arrive back, safe a box for the post office.

Online payments are an excellent way to keep track of your income and obtain your affiliate transfers readily. You might want to look at starting an account with one of the most famous Internet facilities that send and obtain money from this angel.

PayPal is one such service instance. Many individuals are acquainted with PayPal, and everybody understands how to ship money using it. Another common choice is ClickBank, which provides almost identical facilities to PayPal. Both of these options are accurate, fast, and provide economic details that will allow you to catch up with your income readily.

A final instrument to be built up before you embark on your first affiliate marketing program is a promotional scheme for the website where the advertisements will be located. This will imply you have a process in place to link keywords and important sentences back to your site, publish the site on all significant search engines, and also have some material prepared to contribute to the web on a regular basis.

You'll also have at least a few Internet company locations where you can post your URL to company listings. It's essential to make sure that individuals can discover your location during searches; that's where a lot of your traffic comes from. Also, from moment to moment, you want the material to alter mildly, so individuals have a reason to check your location regularly. All of these techniques will improve the chances of clicking on the advertisements published on the page considerably.

Product Choosing

It requires more than just signing up for a program to be effective in affiliate marketing. It also implies going through the method and making sure that you sign up with a program that gives you the chance to earn a bunch of cash.

Here are a few tips to assist you in determining which products would provide you with a strong return on income produced.

When it goes to affiliate marketing, one of the first stuff to believe about is determining where your skills and knowledge lie. One of the keys to choosing the best products has to do with what you learn and how much you understand about it.

For instance, an individual who has been working in telecommunications for a variety of years is likely to learn a lot about telephony, associated facilities, and technology that is being used in that sector.

This would render it a natural fit for telecommunications suppliers, services, suppliers, and retailers to create a website that would create a perfect showplace for advertisements.

Keep in mind that using your information bank will enable you to discover innovative methods to get the correct individuals to your location. In turn, they will be the correct market sector to be interested in advertisements; it greatly improves your likelihood of gaining constant, rewarding revenue.

Another part of setting up the correct goods to support is where you see a niche to fill in. Finding a population or business sector that in the marketing system tends to be largely ignored can provide the impetus you need to create a good affiliate marketing program.

By encouraging yourself and the affiliate advertisements to people and companies that do not receive much attention, you are rapidly building up a position where the rivalry is less ferocious and enhancing your ability to create a safe income stream.

A third strategy is merely looking at what is presently accessible to encourage products. This can be done by reviewing the kinds of promotions provided through the affiliate program.

If you are not particularly interested in promoting with your website, then spend some time searching out the volume and the median income produced by the various sectors depicted in the Internet. There are a range of markets worth considering when you decide to join the affiliate marketing environment. Here are three programs that, merely because of their stabilization and efficiency, caught the attention of many individuals.

ClickBank: http:/www.clickbank.com may be the best known of the three programs.

There are a variety of factors why, when it comes to affiliate programs, individuals consider ClickBank such an appealing option.

One element is that, within two minutes of completion of the transaction, the income produced by any acquisition produced through the ad portal is assigned to your account.

Because ClickBank offers such an extensive monitoring program, affiliates can easily see how things are going, even if various locations are running as a portion of the program.

This handy interface of software means you don't need to set up a separate ClickBank account for every separate program you're working on. Everything can be routed to a core ClickBank account and there will be plenty of transaction details to help you sort the accounts into workable details about how much you do from each website.

You will also have a branded gateway, along with the advertisements on your locations, which will take visitors to the ClickBank marketplace. Any products bought through your gateway on the marketplace will also be subject to a grant payment to you, reflecting in your regular details just as any buy from the affiliate advertisements would. This, in fact, enables you to use the funds that ClickBank offers to maximize your earning potential. Currently, payments are produced through a check, which is sent out every two weeks.

As an affiliate network, www.paydotcom.com is also an outstanding option. Just like with ClickBank, PayDotCom offers an easy-to-use affiliate interface for viewing your figures in real-time. By guiding tourists to the marketplace through the gateway on your website, you can readily monitor information such as the number of clicks on the advertisements and the number of sales you have produced.

One of PayDotCom's benefits is that this program interfaces with your PayPal account, meaning suppliers can directly ship your monthly fee to your PayPal account. It is essential to remember that not all suppliers will use PayPal as a technique of payment, so you can also obtain deposits through check.

Still, PayPal is used by a variety of suppliers, and that can often imply revenue generated without waiting a long time. Keep in mind that you will be subject to any charges you usually incur when getting money if you pick PayPal as your preferred technique of payment.

In the same way, you will also charge PayDotCom a tiny proportion of the payout on each buy. This program is simple to sign up with, and employees do an excellent job of working with people who are new to marketing affiliates.

A third alternative, http:/www.shareasale.com, is quickly gaining acceptance among affiliate marketers. Shareasale is free to participate as an affiliate as a program intended to suit the material of your existing website.

Basically, you can sign up for the program and then browse through a list of available merchant programs, choosing those you think will be of concern to your website readers and viewers. The list of merchants involves a broad range of types and products of the sector, some of which are digital, but many of them are physical.

The sales earnings will differ. Some dealers tend to use a flat rate for a sale, while others go to the buy quantity with a percentage commission. While finding out the merchant register, it is simple to determine which technique is favored.

Individuals who want to look at the merchant list before signing up for the program can search by category, compensation method, and the newest programs that have been added over the last 20 days.

As with all the finest affiliate programs, Shareasale makes it simple to look around the clock at your traffic and earnings. All the reports are web-based, so no special software is needed to load the reports.

You can receive payments on produced income through a check mailed to you or through direct deposit to a bank account. At current, in order to obtain a deposit, you have to earn at least $50.00 USD during the past calendar month. Any sum under that cap will be transferred to the next payment cycle item choices.

As an instance, you decide that as part of your affiliate approach, you may be concerned about encouraging legal facilities. Get some numbers about how much income mediation services and law firms are probable to produce in a year.

If this appears promising, you can create a website that is perfect for advertisements that monitor legal companies, arbitration facilities, and even legal firms ' office equipment. This approach can give rise to some great possibilities for revenue.

It is essential to note that it may take some time to determine which path to follow with your affiliate marketing strategy. While it's true that some individuals enter affiliate programs with a very straightforward view of what they want to do and why, it's not incorrect to take some time to explore your alternatives. Do some research and even get some external views about the opportunities for achievement.

Don't let yourself be discouraged merely because it's not all crystal clear as you start this portion of the method. Practicing some patience and finding the correct products to encourage as part of the program will only help to create you more committed to the program's achievement.

Ultimately, you will discover the products that will contribute to a very effective affiliate marketing scheme and give you not only a beautiful stream of income but also a lot of personal fulfillment.

Benefits of Affiliate Marketing

If you've been considering a marketing affiliate enterprise, there are some very good reasons why you should go with this recurring income generation technique. Here are some of the respects in which affiliate marketing can be a profitable income-generating means that it will be stable and enable you to increase visibility over the moment.

One of the first benefits for the fresh entrepreneur of affiliate marketing is that the start-up costs are very small. Most businesses offering affiliate marketing programs do not require the affiliate to make any kind of financial payment.

Expenses are restricted to what you need to pay to link to the Internet, the software that you may need to add to your desktop, and a website where you can place advertisements related to the affiliate marketing program. With websites hosting such a low-cost service these days, it will be a breeze to set up your own website for affiliate advertisements.

In reality, if you already have a website up and running, you might not have to set up anything. You may already have a website devoted to your interest in alternative fuel alternatives as an instance.

It would be a natural way to gain a little cash to sign up for an affiliate program that places advertisements on your page that click through to companies that generate vegetable-based gas alternatives. One of the simplest ways to create a constant Internet existence that results in a steady flow of revenue is to associate your interests with the topic of the advertisements that appear on your website.

The reality that there are so many distinct kinds of methods to start up the program is another reason that affiliate marketing is such a moneymaker. You can use the pay-per-click option, which performs well when supporting unique deals. Ads that lead to product review pages are often a way for brand consumers to browse your portal and leave remarks about the products they buy.

Using advertisements to redirect to opt-in email sites enables businesses to create qualified email lists to use in their promotions, resulting in revenue for you when individuals choose to sign up. In reality, you could possibly have on your page or blogs a mixture of these and other advertisements, all gaining your cash on an ongoing basis.

A third reason why affiliate marketing is so appealing is that in order to operate with the projects you don't have to work quite your day job. Instead of heading out on a limb with your affiliate company, it's just a question of putting aside a few hours each week to devote yourself to signing up for programs, supporting the websites where the advertisements are supposed to operate and allowing your company to develop.

As affiliate programs get on their feet and start generating decent quantities of income, you can increase the quantity of the moment you spend on the venture, eventually phasing out somebody else's work and generating full-time income flows. This kind of flexibility offers few income possibilities.

Affiliate marketing is not a quick scheme to get wealthy, although the correct programs have plenty of cash to make. The programs will need to be devoted some time and energy.

But the good thing is that once you handle websites and have advertisements put on search engine pages become prominent, you will start to see recurring revenue from your attempts. At the moment, this could result in a very appealing revenue that enables both the resources and the moment.

Disadvantages of Affiliate Marketing

1. From a logical point of view, you will not own any affiliate marketing program. You will just need to use the current ones. You are thus totally dependent on the laws of your merchant and comply with their circumstances. A program that may sometimes appear attractive, may subsequently become less and less competitive, but you're not going to be prepared to modify the terms yourself, all you can do is express the need for further modifications to the discounts on the specified products, etc. And then wait for the merchant to introduce modifications.

2. Depending on the industry, you don't control your competition. Since there are powerful advantages of entering an affiliate company, such as low investment expenses, high-profit prospects, and no need for knowledge, many individuals are trying their hand at affiliate marketing. Practically anyone can participate in and succeed. Highly skilled affiliate marketers from the same niche make up a strong contest, which is a clear threat to your results and a major drawback. That shouldn't fear you, though. Remember that hard work and persistence are the compulsory variables of achievement.

3. The reality is, once a referral has been created, a recurring client will never buy from you again. Naturally, to repeat the acquisition, he will do it straight to the affiliate seller. That's the affiliate company nature. You are committed to repeatedly pursuing fresh leads. Unless you participate in affiliate marketing programs that provide recurrent commissioning.

4. Revenue Guarantee can be a tremendous chance, as well as a major risk. No one guarantees that it will be simple to work as an affiliate marketer, and you will receive the anticipated income immediately. It's a task you're facing and putting all your attempts into maximizing the chance, but all in all, it's hard to imagine how much cash you'll ultimately spend on it.

5. Freelance Jobs are not for everyone to feel happy with such an operating style requires a specific character. It can lead to feeling purple like loneliness or stagnation in some conditions. But there

are ways that such a mental condition can be minimized and overcome. Just don't shut yourself away from individuals at home. Find your workspace outside somewhere and go out there every day.

6. Affiliate marketing is sometimes connected with marketing campaigns for spammy, and that is some reality. Some short-sighted affiliate marketers are everywhere producing spammy and false material and expecting fast and tiny victories. Beware, your days are numbered once you tap into the marketing techniques of black hat affiliates and false advertising. By joining this shady route, you will eventually lose your confidence, and worse, you will jeopardize the reputation of your merchant. In addition, spammy affiliate campaigns lead to the vendor's side breaking up cooperation, and then you're done and can't expect any payment at all. Better concentrate on the long-term affiliate approach and invest in quality rather than amount–this will provide you with viable and recurrent income.

7. While this doesn't happen often, and the vast majority of affiliate marketers won't do it, there are instances of hijacking affiliate connections, so the fraudster receives someone's license.

Then you can hardly get it back. So, you can only hope that you will not be targeted by such an affiliate scam.

Chapter 3: Creating Online Courses

Steps to Create Your Online Courses

1. Set Goals and Objectives

This first step is one of the hardest, but most important, steps you will take. Quite simply, what do you want the students to know? You must decide at this point what you ultimately want the students to know or accomplish when they have completed the course or unit. A basic goal for this project might be: "Students will learn valuable research skills." Often, however, the goal is based on a need something students don't presently know what you would like them to know.

Finally, based on needs, teachers can develop more specific instructional goals. Learning goals are mastered by accomplishing certain objectives. An example of an instructional goal and objectives for this project might be: "Each student will complete a ten-step online orientation and reach 80 percent mastery on the final assessment." Just having a basic understanding of your goals and objectives can help you plan your course by starting with the end (what you ultimately want students to accomplish) in mind. Keep in mind that goals and objectives should be measurable and should answer the following questions.

> What are the educational goals and objectives?
> How will these goals be accomplished?
> Which goals might not be accomplished, and what accommodations can be made for them?
> When students meet goals, are they also meeting standards?
> What information or skills do students need to be able to meet these goals and objectives successfully?
> How much time is needed for goals and objectives to be met?
> How much will this course cost to create? Where will the money come from?

Another tool to help you as you set goals for your online unit is "The Goals Grid," developed by Fred Nickols. Nickols (with a little help from his colleagues) developed the tool to help users achieve goal clarity. By prompting us to perceive the goals you want to achieve as planned, properly structured goals and objectives become better.

The Goals Grid is simply a framework for critically thinking about your intended goals and objectives. Do all of your goals fall into Quadrant II (Avoid) or Quadrant IV (Eliminate)? If so, perhaps you're focusing too much on the negative. On the other hand, if no goals involve these quadrants; perhaps, you're not open-minded or realistic. Finding a balance is key.

Let's use a realistic example from above and work through The Goals Grid together. For example, let's say our goal is: "Each student will complete a ten-step online orientation and reach 80 percent mastery on the final assessment."

	I **Achieve** Ex: 80% Mastery	II **Avoid** Ex: Student Negativity
Do We Have It?	III **Preserve** Ex: High Library Usage	IV **Eliminate** Ex: Special Ed Failures
	Do We Want It?	

The Goals Grid. Created by Fred Nickols

Depending on what you find in your grid exercise, you may want to write other goals based on your findings.

2. Be Aware of the Barriers

Even given all of the advantages to online learning, there are, admittedly, some barriers and hurdles to overcome. By taking a proactive stance, however, the "Three T" barriers (time, technology, and teaching) can easily be overcome.

- **Time**

One of the biggest barriers to face is the amount of time needed to create an online course. Creating an online course is one of the biggest challenges that I have taken on—but also one of the most worthwhile. Keep in mind that, once the course is created, you will be able to save time in the future. You only have to create the course once. While you may (and should) make continual revisions to the course, the biggest chunk of time is in the creation, not the revision. If you take the time now to create a quality, standards-based course, you'll be able to use it for years to come.

- **Technology**

Other than course content, another huge time-taker involves technology. Learning new technology, deciding on course delivery options, and working with your school's technology team to get the course up and running can be extremely time-consuming. Another technology issue is the course upkeep. To be effective, it is critical to keep the course content and site updated. Failing to update the course results in outdated, old (and boring) information—just the opposite of what you intended when you started the process! Finding a competent Web designer will be invaluable to you as you go through this process. Remember, you don't have to have the "techie" skills to create and update the site, but you do have to be able to find the help you need!

- **Teaching with Technology Issues**

In an online course, students are more exposed to:

➢ Internet safety (protecting students from sharing personal information with strangers),

➢ copyright violations (properly citing Internet sources)

➢ classroom management issues

Although it may seem easy to look at online learning as a class by itself (pun intended!), actually online instructional experts say there really should be no difference at all. "A virtual classroom should not be much different from a real classroom—at least, not in the ways that count."

(Porter 1997, 24).

3. Research

This is the time when you will really begin to prepare yourself by researching and reading articles about online training and learning. This is a key time to begin gathering books on teaching with technology and surfing the Internet for related sites.

As you consider the available options, don't forget about the valuable resources in your own building—staff members who may have created, or who may be in the process of creating their own online courses. Ask around—you might be able to learn from their mistakes and expertise!

Another great resource can be found by either physically visiting or virtually visiting a nearby college. Colleges have been using and taking advantage of distance learning opportunities for a number of years now. E-mailing a professor or department chair could prove advantageous as you're digging around for resources. In some cases, you can even virtually "visit" online classrooms by going in as a guest.

By observing how the course is set up, witnessing how the instructor gets students involved, and discovering what types of activities are included in the course, you'll have a better idea of how you want to structure your own course.

Although many other Web sites, books, and articles are surfacing every day, these sources are enough to get you started in the right direction. Just as teachers don't always agree about how best to teach in the "regular" classroom, there are many differing opinions when it comes to teaching online.

The following are five popular myths about online education:

- **Online Learning Is Easy to Evaluate**

Online schools have been in existence for many years now. Although it is difficult to compare online learning directly to a regular school setting, the comparison usually shows a minimal difference in the outcomes. Of course, the convenience of online learning is well documented and can provide success to those who may have been unable to attend regular school.

- **Online Education Saves Teachers Time**

Learning to work with online technology is time-consuming, difficult, and ultimately inconvenient. Some teachers clearly view preparing technologically supported lessons as a much greater demand on their time and energy than preparing a classroom activity without technology. Certainly, time will be saved in the future—once the course is up and running. The grading time alone, for example, will be considerably shortened if automated grading systems are used. But, as stated before, the start-up time is considerable.

- **Online Teaching Equals Better Learning**

Information and communication technology can, and often does, provide a greater number of students with access to information that they may have been unable to access, but this is not to say that students are grasping and understanding the concepts involved. That's why it's critical to put quality evaluative tools in place throughout the unit. What—and how much—students learn is ultimately up to you. That's why an entire chapter here is devoted to course design and another to planning quality instruction.

- **Online Teaching Is Easier Than Traditional Teaching**

Wrong! Just because you don't see your students face-to-face every day doesn't mean this instructional method is any easier than traditional teaching strategies. In fact, online teaching can be harder because building rapport and relationships online take considerably more effort. Some online teachers have reported that, although online teaching is "ten times harder" than classroom teaching, they wouldn't have it any other way.

- **Online Teaching Is Best for Advanced Students**

Wrong again! One of the best things about designing online courses is the ability to differentiate and plan lessons and activities for learners of all ability levels. In my online course, for example, the advanced students completed all ten "Giant Steps," while a basic English course completed seven of the ten steps. As in traditional instruction, sometimes modifications and adaptations are needed.

At a recent technology conference, survey results showed that online student success depends both on reading level and grade point average (GPA). In fact, students who read on grade level (or above) and have at least a 2.5 GPA (C average) tend to be successful. Students do not have to be on the honor roll or have technical supremacy to succeed in an online environment.

4. Look at Other Online Courses

To get acquainted with what's available, take a virtual field trip! Take a look around at other web courses to get some general ideas at this preliminary stage. Some Web courses have restricted access (although most will allow you "in" if you request permission and advise them of your purpose); others have open access, allowing anyone entrance. As you're looking around, don't forget to peek around in your own building—or district—to see what might be going on right next door.

With the increasing popularity of online courses, software programs known as courseware are popping up. Courseware systems provide an Internet-based program to manage all aspects of online education, namely teaching and learning. Some tasks that courseware routinely performs are evaluating and grading, developing course rosters, and tracking course information.

Courseware utilizes tools to facilitate learning by distributing course information, delivering instruction, and facilitating teacher-student interaction.

As you're diving into online courseware, here are some of the best starting points!

Below are the things to note when looking at other online courses:

- **Hardware**
  - ➢ Access to the site requires special facilities.

- Learners with distinct operating systems can access the location using distinct kinds of pcs.
- A dial-up connection is quick enough for the site to operate well.
- Will it need a direct line or a dedicated line in order to function properly?
- A wireless link is sufficiently stable for the site to function well.
- The performance capacity of the computer is needed in order to perform well.
- To access and perform all equipment, the computer does not involve any unique equipment.
- Students can use an elderly PC to finish this course.
- Students can use a brand-new PC to finish this course.

- **Software**
  - Are there any preferred web browsers?
  - Recommended or needed specific variants of any browser(s).
  - You can use any browser to access data about the course.
  - The mode of supplying learners is with the necessary software.
  - Apprentices must offer their own software.

- ➤ The popular software variations needed to complete tasks or use equipment.

- **Operation Policies Set on the Networks**
  - ➤ It seems safe for courses or organizational networks.
  - ➤ It is simple to access courses or organizational networks and function well.
  - ➤ Course locations include claims of confidentiality and safety.
  - ➤ Logging of the institutions' policies on security and privacy.

- **Educational Tools**
  - ➤ Simple to use tools because they enable learners to transfer abilities using comparison websites.
  - ➤ The site will explain and demonstrate new instruments.
  - ➤ Several instruments for asynchronous learning or communication are accessible.
  - ➤ Several instruments for synchronous learning or communication are accessible.

- **Kind of Resources and Media Used**
  - ➤ The course layout incorporates different teaching styles or preferences.

- Multimedia is often used.
- Audio/Video streaming data is accessible.
- You can download materials rapidly.
- The median prints out is a manageable size when text documents are written.
- From the duration of the course and the topic matter, the quantity of related content appears suitable.
- The products are of high quality.
- (Apparently) most of the products were developed by the professor or course planner.
- (Apparently) most of the components were obtained from other sources.
- Information sources are correctly recorded or assigned.
- The sources appear to be existing and precise, representing a range of points of view.
- The data appears to be timely.
- It is possible to reuse the equipment.
- In this course, the products can be used only or only once.
- The internet applications are standing alone, without the need for a handbook, CD, or additional equipment.
- Additional data can be discovered in a handbook, CD, or other formats.

- **Kind and Quantity of Assignments**
  - ➤ Tasks are mentioned in a syllabus or timetable of the course.
  - ➤ The number of tasks appears appropriate for the course's duration and scope.
  - ➤ It seems practical and sensible the amount and sort of tasks per week or teaching module.
  - ➤ Assignment kinds represent distinct styles or preferences of teaching.
  - ➤ Assignments are suitable for learning the topic.
  - ➤ Assignments are suitable for this level of education Real-time and require asynchronous tasks.
  - ➤ Instructions are given for learners to understand how to complete the tasks in what format.
  - ➤ Instructions are supplied so that students understand how to operate the software or instruments to check plagiarism.

- **Required Course Duration**
  - ➤ Learners must finish newspapers, workbooks, essays, study papers, or questionnaires.
  - ➤ Apprentices must take part in chat meetings, conference calls, or video lectures.
  - ➤ Learners must receive a certain amount of e-mails or publish so many remarks on a newsletter panel.

- Apprentices are needed to attend laboratory meetings.
- Throughout the course, learners show their mastery of the topic or ability in several respects.

- **Required Interaction with Fellow Students**
  - Apprentices are needed or motivated to engage in group or project operations.
  - Apprentices are needed or motivated to operate on some or all tasks alone.
  - Outside support is permitted or motivated by mentors, peers, educators, or other learners.
  - Learners are needed outside the school to interview individuals.
  - Interpersonal communication among learners is suggested or needed.
  - There is a need for a specific quantity of communication between the teacher and the learner, and between the learner and others in the school.
  - The response time of the teacher is sensible and coherent.
  - In the course, more than one technique of communication is used.

- **Evaluations**
  - ➤ At the end of the semester, the learners assess the course and the efficiency of training.
  - ➤ Assessments are secret (depending on privacy policy or security policy).
  - ➤ Assessments have finished online and presented.
  - ➤ Evaluations, other than the internet, are finished and presented.
  - ➤ Evaluations involve students to choose from multiple selections or other options mentioned.
  - ➤ Evaluations enable students to comment in writing.
  - ➤ Teachers see the assessments. (Unless it is recorded in a privacy declaration or safety declaration, you may not be willing to know this from the Website).
  - ➤ Assessments are used to enhance the course or curriculum. (If this is not recorded in a privacy declaration or safety declaration, you may not be prepared to know from the Website.)

- **10. Course Duration and Class Size**
  - ➤ The course duration seems suitable for the quantity and quality of the protected data.
  - ➤ The size of the school seems suitable for efficient communication between teachers and learners.
  - ➤ The course duration seems suitable for the quantity of credit provided to the job.

➢ The timeframe for an online course seems suitable.

Decide on Course Content

Planning for online instruction is no different than planning for traditional classroom instruction. You want students to be actively engaged in their learning. To meet this goal, you should plan high quality, interactive lessons that require students to participate and make connections with what they're learning.

Taking the time to plan quality, interactive lessons are critical to a successful online course. For starters, plan an activity that helps students get to know each other—and you! One possibility is having students make an ID badge for themselves that they post online for others to view. The ID badge would contain the student's picture, e-mail address, and hobbies (adding the hobbies feature allows opportunities for student connections). Another opening activity is to get students used to online discussion boards by playing, "Did I Lie?" To participate, students make up a crazy statement about themselves. Other students have to decide whether or not the statement is true.

Now that the students have gotten to know each other, it's time to plan your content-related lessons. You've decided on the what—now it's time for the how. How are you going to get students to learn (or master) the content? Whatever you do, don't make the same mistake I made and give too much discussion in the form of text. Text without graphics, movement, and activity is just like a teacher lecturing without stopping. And, what's worse, students don't even have the instructor to zone out on! You hear the words (or see the words in this case), but don't understand a thing. This can be true for online lessons—if you're not careful. For Giant Step 3, for example, I asked students to find three online database articles.

Including fun and excitement in your course or orientation is not to say that every lesson must be a fun-filled learning adventure. Rather, the point I'm trying to make is that a variety of instructional strategies should be used—both asynchronous and synchronous lessons, cooperative and individual activities, and short-term and long-term projects. You may also wish to choose a "hybrid" option that has proven to be very successful. The hybrid option includes a mix of online instruction and regular face-to-face meetings. The regular meetings are a helpful checkup at which the teacher can answer questions and clarify specific details and requirements.

Another reason it's important to include interactive assignments while you're planning your online unit is to avoid the isolation that can sometimes occur with Web-based instruction. By planning interactive assignments, you force students to communicate with each other on a regular basis.

No matter what learning activities you've planned, it is important to provide a course syllabus or outline for students to follow. When planning your course, it is important that your course

"RISE" to the occasion:

R = RELEVANCE

a) Show how instruction relates to the learner.

b) Be an instructor who models lifelong learning.

c) Build a strong relationship between course objectives and outcomes.

d) Teach in a problem-based manner that applies knowledge to real-world applications.

I = INTEREST

a) Vary content organization and presentation to avoid boredom.

b) Use active voice and action words.

c) Provide opportunities for students to interact with each other and you, the instructor.

d) Use debate to get students actively involved.

e) Utilize different learning styles.

f) Encourage healthy competition between students.

S = SATISFACTION

a) Provide opportunities for students to use new skills.

b) Provide continual and timely feedback and reinforcement to learners.

c) Provide ample positive feedback.

d) Share exemplary work with students.

E = EXPECTANCY

a) Make the course easy to navigate.

b) Organize the text for easy readability.

c) Follow good graphic and design principles (keep it simple, easy to navigate, user-friendly with color and lots of white space).

d) Be explicit and upfront regarding expectations of student participation and assignment quality (adapted from Lynch 2001, 21).

Advantages and Disadvantages of Online Courses

Advantages of Online Courses

Increased Access

Because online learning can take place anywhere and anytime, this reason alone often accounts for the ever-increasing popularity of distance learning. Space and time barriers are instantly removed, allowing greater access for students with jobs, extracurricular activities, and busy schedules. Students have virtual access to up-to-date content and learning 24 hours a day!

Limited Staffing

Even with limited staffing, the online unit allows a few teachers to reach all students and teach valuable research and library-related lessons—something that cannot be achieved using the traditional "face to face" method.

An Increase in Student Enrolment

As a result of the unlimited reach, online courses offer, you are able to have many students from all over the world without increasing the teaching resources, and therefore your business venture is more profitable.

Increased Staff

As you would expect, a larger student population leads to a larger teacher population. With almost 30 full-time English teachers, there is no way that I could physically meet the orientation needs of every class. Even if every English teacher brought his or her students to the media center for a week-long orientation and research unit, I'd never survive—and we'd have to increase the school year to do it!

Increased Availability

Once an online unit has been created, other schools can use and even modify the content or material. Collaboration can take place, allowing more than one school to take advantage of already-created online instructional units and teach students as they move through the school system.

Increased Awareness

Since I've started this unit, I now have administrators, teachers, parents, and students who understand that library standards and critical information skills exist and really matter. In addition, all parties involved now see me in a teaching role, and there is more support as a result.

Increased Motivation

Like it or not, students love to use computers! Students who would normally have behavior problems now are more actively involved in their learning. Even though some of the same information is taught, learning online is more user-friendly and interesting to students.

Disadvantages of Online Courses

1. Lack of accreditation and low quality. Check that the program is certified and check this data with the accrediting agency before you register in any online course. Legitimate schools are proud of their status with accrediting organizations, from existing universities to new online colleges, and organizations are pleased to accredit excellent schools. This data is, therefore, easily accessible for you to search online. If you graduate from a non-accredited college, you may discover yourself with a meaningless degree that will leave you in debt and not better ready for the workplace. Verifying the accreditation of an online program is a

small step that in the long run, can save you time, money, and heartbeat.

2. While this may seem apparent, learners tend to underestimate the effect of never meeting in the school with the teacher and other learners. In a Time Opinion piece, Mark Edmundson, an English professor at Virginia University, stated that online education produces a "monolog and not a true dialog" in the teaching setting. Building interactions in an internet setting will involve more effort with your teacher and students.

3. Typically, more work online courses involve more reading and tasks than traditional classes. Overall, programs improve the performance of their online courses, which implies learners will have to do more to demonstrate they have learned the stuff. Expect to spend on each online course at least 10 hours a week. However, requiring 15 or 20 hours per week for a single course is not unusual.

4. Intense self-disciplinary obligation Online courses generally have timetables for tasks, exams, lecture comments, etc. That's not the issue. The issue is the time management and organizational abilities needed to remain on top of your job, allocating an adequate quantity of time to finish each assignment, and balancing your course work against other life objectives. If you tend to procrastination, you may need to reinforce your skillset before selecting a course or program online.

5. Traditional college programs typically give or even require learners to coordinate with consultants to assist them in scheduling their college route. If you need only one or two courses, this is not a problem. If you are studying a full degree online, however, you will need to be proactive in discovering the data you need to make sure you take the correct courses for your degree scheme. Straying from this route may be a failure to make scholarly advancement, and you may find it difficult to secure economic assistance.

Chapter 4: Social Media Influencer

According to Tapscott, social media began in early 2007 as a means of sharing, socializing, collaborating, and peering. Social media can be defined as an online community building and maintenance, sharing and production of collaborative information, and generation, transmission, and intake of user-generated content. As of 2018, there were 3 billion social media users in the world, and the Millennials in this group devote about 25% of their time to their social media accounts, thus making social media advertising a rapidly growing industry.

Who is a Social Media Influencer?

An influencer is a person who has the power to sway or influence the decisions of their followers because they have expertise in a particular area, and their followers trust them. Social media influencers usually have many people following them, and these followers pay close attention to the influencer's point of view. This gives them the power to convince people to purchase things, and this perfectly positions a social media influencer as a good marketing tool and brand ambassador for their products.

Various brands around the world are using brand ambassadors as a mode of getting their products to the hearts of their customers and prospective customers. This has become a very lucrative source of income for social media influencers as some people usually charge up to $25,000 for a single promotional post. This has made many people want to venture into this venture. Due to the rush for money, many people do not do their research properly and end up having a mammoth task making this venture work. As we saw in chapter one, it is important to do proper planning before starting up a project. So, here are a few things many people do not do.

1. Many people hardly take the time to choose their niche. In this case, it should be a topic that they are knowledgeable and passionate about, and this is their ideal niche. This way, they will be doing something that they love, and it will be easier for them to keep their followers interested.

2. Just visiting any blogging or social media platform, creating an account and posting your content there simply does not cut it in becoming a successful social media influencer. It is important for you to take time to figure out the medium or platform they would like to use to engage their audience.

3. A profile bio is not like a resume that should be official and straight to the point. You need to keep it fresh, creative, and relatable to your targeted niche market. The profile bio tells the world who you are and if you keep the bio

interesting, more followers will be interested in following you.

4. One pos a month will not make an impact in the social media realm. The Internet is the information superhighway, and information is generated in real-time. It is, therefore, necessary for you to keep your content current and futuristic so as to keep your audience interested. Remember also to post frequently because as the saying goes, out of sight out of mind.

5. Do not just post content on the Internet so that the audience can just read it, post it to tell a story. Irrespective of whether it is a photo post, video, or text post, you will connect more with your audience when they relate to your message.

6. Content generation is done by millions of other Internet users and bloggers worldwide, but what separates social media influencers from users is the fact that the content put out by the influencer is more visible to audiences globally than for a majority of other users. In order to achieve this, you have to make sure that your content is trending, you have used the right hashtags, your titles are catchy, and have done just the right marketing to them if need be.

7. If you do not have the virtue of patience, then social media influencing is no the game for you. It takes time, patience, creativity, and persistence to become a successful social

media influencer. Gaining followers that belief in you is not an easy feat and never happens overnight. Patience is, therefore, a key virtue in the social media influencing industry

Why Should You Become a Social Media Influencer?

You are on the right track if you are considering venturing into social media influencing. It is an amazing, empowering, and fulfilling venture. Companies all over the world are continually increasing their social media marketing budgets, and if you properly position yourself, you would gain a lot financially. You may have seen a couple of social media influencers eating expensive food or even traveling first class around the world on the promoter's bill, just to name a few opportunities.

Living the lifestyle of the digital nomad could appeal to you for different reasons. In other words, constructing a personal brand and freeing up your artistic abilities allows you to be your own boss. Perhaps even quitting that 9-5. If you want to become an influencer, there are many distinct motivations. When finding out your personal brand and photography style, knowing your main goals is vital.

It may surprise you, however, that not everyone in this sector who produces it initially planned to become an influencer of social media. The transition from Instagrammer to an influencer is entirely organic for many social media stars. These unintentional influencers started with a hobby at first, and they were taken by surprise by the spectacular development of the crowd.

Understanding Social Media Influencer Marketing

Everyone who works hard to become a social media influencer invests a lot in terms of time and resources to become a success, and just like in any business, an investment needs an even greater return for it to be worth it. Being that social media influencers are also brands; they need to learn how to go about influencer marketing in order to monetize their brand.

Influencer marketing can be defined as a partnership between social media influencers and brands or companies where the former can create and raise awareness of the latter's brand, service, or product. This awareness is, in most cases, necessary when a company is launching a product or wants to create brand credibility and recognition.

In general, it basically involves social media influencers creating content about a particular service or product. The most important thing to observe here is that you need to be quite aware and clear of what the brand's marketing objectives are and what they also expect to achieve in terms of their social media influence marketing objectives.

Discussing any topic requires to start with a concept, and so here's the one for marketing social impact: social impact marketing is a method which makes use of the social media (content generated by individuals on a daily basis using extremely available and accessible systems such as blogs, groups, wikis, and other social media networks) and social influence.

The definition warrants further clarification. Social media relates to material that regular people create for and consume. It involves the remarks that an individual contributes to a website at the start of an essay, the household pictures that he uploads to a photo-sharing site, the talks he has with colleagues in a social network, and the blog entries he writes or remarks about. That's social media, and it makes a product publisher and arbitrator for everyone around the globe.

Social media influencing is mainly about identifying, accounting, and making the best of the fact that for a potential customer to make a purchase, either online or offline, they are influenced by the people and content that they engage in with their social circles. This is achieved by people sharing their opinions on social media platforms and consuming the material other people post.

Social Media Influence Fundamentals

In order to understand the workings of social media influence, you cannot ignore considering how people are swayed in everyday life. Social influence was in existence long before the Internet was in existence as people would consult their friends and family when it came to decisions on what to buy. What someone purchased would influence the buying decision of the other person. In short, word of mouth is the oldest form of social influence.

Positive influence is not bad, and most of the time, people will always look for it. It is natural for people to ask each other for advice, make decisions together with friends, family, and workmates. The level at which someone is influenced depends on a number of varying conditions. When someone is buying products that have a low consideration, more often than not, no form of consultation is made.

This is because there are aa lot of similar products available to choose from, like toothpaste or sugar. These goods are also of a low price, and therefore they do not carry a lot of risks. A car on the other end is a product that has a high consideration. Let alone the cost of buying it, the maintenance costs that accrue while operating a vehicle is on the higher side. A lot of consultation is therefore made before making such a purchase because it carries with it a much larger risk.

Social influence is significant to every purchase made, but it matters more when high consideration purchases are made. This is because the customer feels like they can make better and more informed decisions when making their purchases simply because they value the understanding and advice of the people that made similar decisions before them.

Qualities of a Successful Social Media Influencer

Be Authentic

Authenticity is essential for social media influencer focusing on fashion marketing. This research described authenticity as the influencer with her adherents being authentic, frank, and open. Authenticity enables an influencer to relate on a fresh level to supporters and helps build a connection between supporters and brands. Authentic YouTube content creation provides influencers the chance to communicate their private ideas, views, and style with their supporters who may follow their direction.

Be Confident

Brands want influencers who are confident in themselves to promote their products. It also encourages trust in the brand when influencers convey trust in themselves. This brand confidence leaves followers with a lasting impression and makes them consider becoming a product consumer. "51 percent of marketers think they get stronger clients from influencer marketing, according to the Influencer Orchestration Network. That's because the connection started with the influencer's confidence

Be Interactive

Traditional marketing strategies influencing public relations use press outlets to achieve audiences such as journals, television, and radio. In terms of growing brand awareness, these traditional strategies can be effective, but do not necessarily generate a connection between the brand and customers as social media influencer marketing does today. Influencers shed a favorable light on brand products through interactive video material and encourage their supporters to buy a product and experience it themselves.

Becoming a Social Media Influencer

According to AdWeek magazine, the social media influencer industry will be worth $10 billion by the year 2020. At the same time, handbag manufacturer Oscar De La Renta announced that their turnover doubled when they incorporated social media influencers in their marketing strategy.

It is quite undeniable that the social media industry is only growing stronger and that the influencers are here to stay. Some YouTube influencers like Zoella from Britain get more than 3 million views on a number of the videos they post on YouTube and therefore, it is easy to see why brands are increasingly turning to social media influencers for their social media marketing needs.

So, this begs the question, how does someone become a social media influencer? Since it is an industry that is ever-growing, it can be quite crowded, but it does not mean that it is not possible to get into the influencer market and make an impact. As you work on becoming an influencer in the social media spectrum, below are a few pointers you need to focus on.

Find a Niche Market

We have already established that the influencer market is quite crowded, and the plain truth is that it is only going to get more crowded. You will need to find that conducive corner of the Internet where you are going to make a mark or create that space where you are going to make a name for yourself.

To make the most out of your venture, you will need to discover that niche where you can comfortably create a strong foundation for your social media brand. You, however, have to be careful not to end up in a niche that is not popular because since there is little to no audience, you are bound not to make any money in this niche. The trick is to find a middle ground where you feel comfortable and happy. In short, take time to look for your voice and once you find it, make sure that you do not deviate from it.

Grow Your Personal Brand

You need to constantly work on it by doing extensive research in order to identify the things you need to get things started. Take time to research that niche you have identified and find out important information about the industry like the main influencer in the niche, the brands engaging with that particular niche and also the influencers in it. Most importantly, take time to identify any gaps that exist in the niche market and figure out ways in which you can stand to take advantage of them in building your brand and your niche.

Envision how you want your brand to look like in a couple of years. Use this vision to figure out how you are going to make an entry in the market, and create your content strategy, your brand, and the tone of your voice around this.

Build a Universal Presence

Once you have come up with proper strategies for building your brand, you need to decide the social media platforms you are going to engage with, and then go ahead and create the appropriate social media accounts and profiles. It is very important that you take time to go through each social media platform and understand how it works before you start formulating a strategy. Here, you will consider issues such as the optimum time to send outposts on the various platforms, the type of images or videos that receive more views or user engagement, and so on.

It is advisable to concentrate on a few platforms that you feel comfortable with and make sure you are consistent and aggressive in engaging your audience in terms of posting content and responding to their post comments and feedback. It will be easier to build your brand in such a platform than wasting your time and resources on platforms you are not completely comfortable with.

After you have decided on the platform(s) that you feel most comfortable with, you can now proceed to establish a consistent brand across various platforms. You need to ensure that the social media handles you use are the same across all social media platforms you choose to use. This will make it far much easier for your followers to find you and your content across the different platforms you are present in.

Post your Material

After creating a unified brand presence across the various social media platforms, it is time now to publish your content and start building on your social networks. Do your studies into which content kinds operate best on different platforms?

Images are optimal across Facebook, Twitter, and Instagram in distinct dimensions. In order to function best through Instagram tales or Facebook, videos need to be edited in distinct respects. When uploaded straight to Facebook, Facebook clips operate better than an internal connection. These are all useful suggestions that will assist you when you post to build a dynamic social presence.

Research that hashtags get a bunch of communication, and make sure that they function in your messages. Jump to trendy subjects to become important and get more eyes on your messages. Publish your material, study continuously, and adapt to each platform.

Portray Your Personality

As an influencer of social media, your character is your greatest asset.

Consumers don't essentially always turn to influencers to identify shiny product adverts, but instead, prefer real and frank assessments of stuff they might want to buy for themselves. When they are relatable, influencers are most effective, which is why your character is a significant instrument to build your brand. Start working on how to best communicate with yourself, instead of focusing on professionalism

Be true to yourself and be proud of who you are. Inspire people who want to listen to your voice to follow you. By understanding your honesty, your target audience will think your point of view as an impact if you tackle yourself in a way that you understand is relevant to yourself.

Interact with Your Followers

One of the most important things to a social media influencer is the relationship they have with their followers. It has to be nurtured and grown, and thus you just can't post content and leave their comments and concerns unanswered. The main in terms of collaboration is a two-way road, and building a room where your content can be engaged, trusted, and enjoyed is vital to your achievement as a social media influence.

Network

Networking in social media is the simplest way that someone can use to understand themselves, and this can be achieved both digitally and personally. You may try using apps such as individually to see what occurs in your local area to other freelancers, businessmen, or even electronic or social media? Pop along, engage, encourage yourself, and in the future, generate an extremely helpful contact culture.

It is time for you to introduce yourself to the digital community that you are aspiring to enter. Follow your chosen industry's fellow influencers and businesses, adopt anyone who wishes to follow you, explore what Twitter group chats are going on and involve yourself on a weekly basis, participate in Instagram hashtags, join Facebook organizations and promote your content in any way you can. You need to think in your brand and transmit that in order to get off the floor, so make an attempt and you'll start to see your networking bring in some good money.

Be Consistent

Consistency is one of the most significant elements to be an influencer. Post to all platforms you have chosen to engage on a regular basis. If you're blogging, keep posting there. Be ready to continue filming videos if you're on YouTube. It is crucial for you to be consistent because the content you post on your social networks will have a short shelf life with computational complexity and the rapid growth of timelines for social media. Get more people to view your online content by being consistent—and this is also a nice way to attract the attention of customers!

Be Patient

Being a patient is an ability you need to understand if you want to become a social media influencer. The extra effort is never full of competition, so you're going to have to build a thick skin to get any attention in the social networking arena and get ready to get the graft in.

Get a Website or Blog

While social media is a cheap and amazing mode of getting noticed and will be your main instrument as an influencer, you need to get a blog or website in order to give your business a professional outlook, generate an outstanding Internet existence and have a higher opportunity of attracting visitors.

While you might believe a professional-looking website or blog could cost you a high price, blog pages such as WordPress offer a wide variety of free templates that you can customize to fit your needs, allowing you to create something that looks sleek and fits your branding needs without a budget.

You can also use several distinct widgets and applications to add a free-of-charge tech-savvy component to your blog. Of course, you can branch out and get a builder to help you generate something interesting when you purchase a website builder at a small fee.

A blog or website is an excellent location to record your material, it enables you to generate material that is mildly more evergreen and is not going to vanish as quickly as possible on social media, and it also provides you something concrete to demonstrate any products or potential supporters as a technique of marketing and advertising to reflect what you are attempting to do.

For each dollar they spend on influencer advertising, brands receive an average of $7.65, as indicated by Influencer Marketing Hub. Therefore, it is no surprise that many companies are assigned a particular budget to operate with influencers. Getting savvy is the simplest way to get outside of old school networking to the products you want to cooperate with.

This implies keeping up strategies and methods such as SEO on social media.

Search Engine Optimization is the practice of ranking your blog or website within the search outcomes of Google so that clients can find appropriate keywords when looking for your material.

Implementing your blog or website's fundamental SEO approach could be a sure way to boost your traffic and start building your community as an influencer.

Using the free Internet tools that discuss social media websites and how to get the best out of them will assist you in bringing professional products that use strategies to boost commitment. Be knowledgeable, be forward-thinking, and never attempt to prevent studying, and you will see the cementing of your location of influence.

Use Analytics

This is probably the most significant point of all, and one of the products that will assist you become a social media influencer in your search. You can access a range of analytical instruments to make you a more effective influencer in social media when you understand how to use them.

If you host your Website on a platform such as Blogger or WordPress, data will be included, which can be used to show you which articles are the most famous and which content is not so well done. This is your most important information as an influencer of social media.

If you do not know the crowd, what they like, what they do not like, and how everyone is working best for you, all of the advice listed above will not be particularly efficient.

Notice what kinds of material are working properly and use it to create a forward-looking approach that offers your audience more than they wish.

You can also subscribe to your blog or website instruments like Google Analytics. You will be given data about the kinds of locations that click on their content, how long individuals stay on each web page, how client travel shifts from page to page, how many significant statistics assist you in becoming an influencer.

Nearly every platform has an integrated analytical feature in social media that helps you know what you write. If there are the biggest times to comment about Twitter, how many individuals comment on your Facebook messages, and what hashtags are your fingertips, you can see which material is appreciated the most. Twitter, Facebook, and Instagram have great insight tools, including a weekly check-in and information to support progress.

Make a Plan

While your content is personal, real and linked to itself—it's important also that you plan for tracking, cohesive and producing your product—all the main aims of establishing your platform as an influencer in social media.

Make a scheme for how many times you want to post, what materials you want to deal with, and when you want to post them. Determine any seasonal operations you would like to deal with while maintaining an eye on national days can help you keep ahead of the curve and schedule a regular campaign.

Make sure your system is up to date for a minimum of one month, to allow you to build your brand with lots of signed material and a coherent framework. You will become an influencer of the social media industry if you fit in with all the earlier points in this document.

Advantages and Disadvantages of Social Media Influencing

Advantages of Social Media Influencing

Good Source of Passive Income

Social media influencers are constantly being tracked down by brands and other companies to promote their brands. For social media marketing, the content being sort after here is not strenuous. It could be as simple as posting a photo or a short video (usually 30 to 60 seconds for many big social media platforms and infomercials for YouTube influencers) with the merchandise being promoted or posting a blog post reviewing the product.

For these simple tasks, social media influencers get paid with gift hampers, the merchandise in question (may range from a smartphone to a car), others get paid in hard cash, and other promoters pay both in cash and merchandise. Whatever the payment you receive, you are better off financially or materially than before you sent out that post.

Open to Many Opportunities

As a social media influencer, you are open to many opportunities to make money away from the social media scene. This is because you have a strong following that is willing and available to engage, interact, or listen to you and your views in real life. For example, someone who blogs about fashion may be invited for a talk show by a media station. This way, your followers get to have a personal bond with you, and you are bound to gain many more followers and grow your brand even more.

Work from Anywhere

Once the promoters have given you the content, they want you to post and also their terms and objectives, you are free to carry out the promotion from anywhere at your own convenience. Be it while you are at your day job, at home, while at the beach, you name it. The important thing here is getting the job done.

Disadvantages of Social Media Influencing

Takes Time and Poor Pay

It takes a lot of time, dedication, and resources to become a social media influencer. Many people who set out to this venture give up along the way, and for the few who do not, they have to contend getting paid very discouraging wages or in some cases, they do not get paid entirely.

Extreme Requests/Demands from Promoters

Sometimes promoters ask the social media promoters to market their products in a way that may be uncomfortable, like a promoter asking a fashion blogger taking a photo while wearing a very revealing garment.

Biased Opinions

Some promoters may give social media influencers the condition of giving a biased review for a product to boost sales this is disadvantageous because when your audience realizes you deceived them, you will lose all credibility and eventually your brand will collapse.

Long-term Prospects

The social media influencer industry is highly dynamic and ever-growing. There are many influencers who have taken years to build their brands only for it to collapse overnight. It is very volatile and rapidly growing that if you do not keep yourself ahead of the competition and keep up with the trends in your niche market, you will quickly grow irrelevant and consequently the business you receive will reduce and eventually disappear.

Chapter 5: Membership Websites

There are many distinct methods to make money online (which is a component of why if you're just getting started, it can be so overwhelming). And affiliation pages are preferred by marketers who are online. With a subscription page, you will solely give some kind of material, goods, or facilities to individuals who have paid for accessing your site. And it will also require a regular fee to keep the membership active. There are a number of factors we're going to get into in just a moment to like the membership model, but it is important to dwell deeper into the topic because there are some major obstacles to getting achievement with a membership page.

Many websites now have a region protected by a part of membership only. This is a very good idea because it implies that you can have free tourists that you can attract with an assortment of exciting and valued items and then recommend that they can get your site's complete advantages and save cash by participating for a nominal fee.

This can be a very strong way of generating internet revenue and running a service-based company. If you have your members subscribe to either a monthly or annual membership package to access a password-protected area where exclusive material is made available and you give exceptional value and a wide base of concern (or a specialized niche) to maintain your customers comfortable and want to spread your company to others by word of mouth (one of the most productive ways of developing an online business)

One of the other advantages of a membership page is that without it being completely full, you can start or start your page. In reality, you can allow it to develop organically with material from your clients by creating only a tiny part of your real content. This can be an enormous advantage, and you will be paid in advance. This offers you the advantage of getting a website that has content that individuals really want, you get quality, real-time reviews that help you create a product or service-based website that provides content that your customers want, and not just a website that has things you believe or imagine they might want.

People often waste a ton of time, energy, and money building a fantastic site that no one really likes, so no one will settle for it. The mysteries of internet marketing are to provide relevant data that individuals want at an inexpensive cost and in an easy to discover and comprehend the format, but it must be user-friendly and simple. The simpler, the better because if you complicate things, people won't bother.

Selling software can be one of the most lucrative passive revenue sources you can attempt. Many people don't think about it because they don't have the experience or technical skills like programming, or the ability to write distinct kinds of software, but this is not essential. The reason is that all this can be accomplished without much troubled by other people that you can locate on the internet. It becomes simple once you discover a good creator of the program and have a good idea (this is the significant component). If you can find a small but very useful product or service in an area that needs to be addressed and offer a solution to what's needed, the software you are developing doesn't have to be costly or feature-rich in order to succeed. Often a tiny instrument that solves a large need can be very profitable, if it's priced correctly, going home on the net to those 3.5 billion individuals (plus an expected additional 3 billion over the next few years). If you can get $1 from 0.001 percent of those individuals, you might get a $35,000 return, and if you can make that a recurring payment, it will be very lucrative.

Website Services Everybody starts a website or webpage nowadays, whether using a home desktop PC, a laptop, or a handheld device, most individuals are not technically skilled. In reality, most are questioned technically. There are 101 things to do when setting up a website or page, including all sorts of setups, programming, and little tricks to know if you want things to look perfect. It is impossible for most people to be disturbed and would be willing to pay someone to do it for them.

If you have any skill in setting up websites and anything associated with developing websites like SEO, post writing, producing graphics, developing website themes, programming, etc., then you can readily sell your products to people who want them. Upwork, Freelancer, or some of the other virtual assistant's locations are places to discover these people.

Types of Membership Websites

There are simply several distinct kinds of affiliation pages, but they are typically all lumped together in one large category. The purpose of this chapter of the paper is to demonstrate that when beginning and handling a subscription page, there are some choices. Here we are going to look at some of the most popular kinds of affiliation locations, for sure there are many other opportunities available. With a little bit of innovation, you may figure out other different perspectives.

Information

This is most likely the most popular form of membership websites found on the internet. Members would pay a continuing premium (often a monthly or annual premium) for accessing some sort of exclusive material or data with this sort of blog. In certain instances, this kind of content may be presented in written form, audio, or audio-visual forms. For example, you can either purchase a monthly or an annual subscription when you visit Lynda.com and are interested in watching educational videos that inform you on various topics of interest to you.

Forums

There are virtually hundreds of online forums available online which address on literally any topic you can think of. Many of these forums are free for use by all because they do not charge members anything to open an account and take part in the discussion. There are some other forums, however, that only offer their content to members and restrict participation to members only. These forums usually have a standard monthly or annual fee that is charged at the beginning of the period.

Downloadable Resources/Products

This kind of platform enables you to download various digital products or services from paying respondents. Typically, respondents will be implemented commonly to remain engaged, new products, or property. Members may earn a monthly or annual discount to log in and download the products to the platform. Many online stores that offer WordPress templates provide either a monthly or annual membership option which gives members the chance to access the premium content. Among the pioneers were elegant themes, and many other marketplaces also adopted this model. At Elegant Themes, you can pay an annual bonus and have access to more than 80 different WordPress subjects. There are also many locations providing subscriptions for stock photography. Because they add new products to their inventory almost on a daily basis, the significance of this membership is steadily increasing.

Insider Access

This kind of page is kind of similar to websites linked to information membership, but with some new twist. Members would pay an ongoing price for accessing a website where they would have access to some kind of news/reporting/gossip/rumor. There are a few sports industry cases. ESPN Insider offers attendees access to "exclusive expert evaluation and predictive tools." Rivals.com is yet another example in the sports industry, which gives members a chance to pay for a subscription, either monthly or annually, for insider access to breaking news to issues like news from your favorite football college team.

Services

Service-related websites can also be set up to help installations based on affiliation. Members would be provided access for a monthly or annual payment to some kind of service. An example is the WP Curve that provides a monthly payment for WordPress assistance and assistance to members/customers. You may have read or heard known marketers recommending membership sites as an outstanding way to generate internet money. Here's a look at some of the proprietors of subscription sites or the pros of executives.

Offer Long-term Options

Other than simply having recurring subscription options that run for short periods of less than a year, offer your customers quarterly or biannual subscriptions in place of monthly or life-long membership options on top of annual. For instance, you may charge $25 quarterly instead of $10 monthly. Many customers would prefer this because they save $5 when they take the longer subscription. Lifelong membership could be disadvantageous for you because you will never expect that client to pay for that particular service ever again. It, however, works in some instances.

If you offer clients an alternative to signing up for a shorter period of time, it will be crucial that the subscription for the longer term is discounted so that it can be an incentive for the client to opt for the subscription. Like the example, we have just had a look at earlier. The higher the discount offered for the long-term subscription, the more incentive new respondents will need to sign up for it.

It is usually cheaper, collecting one large payment as compared to several small ones. Long-term memberships obtained in advance also gives you more money instantly, instead of waiting for smaller amounts to trickle in every other month. You can invest this money in ensuring that the content you are offering is important, current, and adding value to your members, resulting in even more sign-ups.

Offer Different Membership Levels

One good way to boost your income is to give higher rates to the members who want to go beyond the regular subscription or want premium or special services that are specific to their needs. Of course, not all your members are going to choose a higher affiliation rate, but some of them are, and that can create a big distinction. You will need a convincing justification for registering for the higher membership level in order to be effective. Again, advanced subjects are a good example. You can subscribe to a normal subscription for an annual fee of $68, or you can choose to add an extra $30 annually for the subscription of an advanced learner and receive certain extra advantages.

Start Low

When it comes to pricing, you will want to give it a lot of attention because it can be a bit difficult to produce future price modifications. It is recommended that you begin with a low subscription fee because it is simpler to raise subscription rates than to reduce the rates. You will face some issues linked to the way you handle your current subscribers if you choose to sell your subscription too quickly and you decide to reduce your rates after a year. Details of a repetitive transaction cannot be modified after it has been set up with several repeated payment providers (including PayPal). Therefore, you have to cancel their present recurring billing and have them register at the reduced cost if you want to reduce the rate your present members' fee. You will most likely lose some members if you do, as not all of them will make an effort or choose to register again, even if the costs are lower. The alternative is a reduction in the subscription rates for your new customer's rates and maintains high subscription fees for your existing subscribers. This is not advisable because your current clients may be upset and add to a range of cancellations. New subscribers are much easier to increase in numbers. If most affiliate venues increase prices, the increase shall not affect present individuals who will continue paying the subscription cost they paid when they were joining your website. This implies, if you raise rates, the older customers will make you less but will also provide them with an incentive to remain active with their membership. If they cancel their membership and decide to return at a later date, they will subscribe and pay the current higher subscription fees. You also have the opportunity to develop your client base more quickly and create an image in the niche or sector before cost increases by starting at a lower price. Again, this is a lovely example of elegant themes. When they started, Elegant Themes charged an annual fee of $19 for membership. The cost of fresh subscribers has since risen to $49 a year and eventually rose to $69 per year as the number of people in its compilation grew, and as its reputation in the WordPress society evolved. The designers also began providing membership for a one-time fee of $249 per year and lifetime membership.

Offer Alternative Payment Options

Based on the high number of ineffective recurring deals through PayPal, it would be better to allow clients to sign up and settle through some other processor than PayPal with a credit card. It would still be advisable to have PayPal among your list of options as it is the most popularly used online payment platform available and some customers like to use it, but also offering other gateways for processing the payments could contribute to more effective for recurring payments.

Advantages and Disadvantages of Creating Membership Websites

Advantages of Creating Membership Websites

Recurring Income

This is greatly the major motivator of why people create affiliate sites. Rather than buying an item and receiving a one-time deposit from a client, you will be charged each month or year (or at another period) with a good subscription portal as soon as that employee is present. If clients have a convincing reason to maintain their affiliation active and continue to pay those charges, the median customer's valuation may be quite large.

Income Predictability

Another reason to enjoy affiliation pages is that they can provide a high amount of predictability or revenue stabilization. As your platform expands and you continue to grow a strong base of paying participants, you can calculate statistics such as the level of customer retention, and this way you will have a more accurate estimate of the duration that an average subscriber remains active. The average amount of fresh customers that sign up per month can also be calculated. With this data, you can estimate relatively correctly how much month-to-month income your location will produce.

Long-term Growth

While affiliation pages offer recurring revenue possibilities and elevated revenue potential, they are usually quite tough at the start. Unless you currently have a platform that you can use to promote your subscription page, obtaining fresh customers can be a task at first. The repeated earnings, however, makes it very feasible for you to be able to develop that revenue over a period of moment continuously. If you can get fresh customers to register at a greater pace than the cancellation rate, you should have a fairly continuous rise in your revenue. A subscription page is one of the finest designs to have a continuously growing revenue through a blog with the required job and energy.

High Customer Value

The charges paid by subscription applications will obviously differ from one location to the next based on the information of what participants are receiving and the target audience. But a website that maintains a member for more than 180 days will generate a higher income per client than would be feasible by selling a similar item at a one-time premium. One of the greatest methods to boost the revenue you earn through establishing a business online is to concentrate on raising each client's quantity you receive, rather than just attempting to achieve more fresh customers. This is made possible by a membership page by retaining paying participants and even encouraging them to upgrade to more premium packages.

Disadvantages of Creating Membership Websites

There are also some important difficulties or disadvantages, and I believe they are ignored on many occasions when discussing affiliation applications. I've taught some stuff the hard way, so if they can assist you, I'd like to talk about the difficulties.

1. The biggest disadvantage of membership websites is that most people just don't want to sign up for repetitive payments. Customers are of course prepared to register fora recurring payment if it is in their best interest to do so, but the offer has to be extremely convincing and a clear advantage to be received.

Most people are concerned by the fact that they may forget to cancel the recurring payment and end up being charged for something they don't want or use. It is much simpler to purchase products that only require one-time payment and in certain instances, identical products on a subscription basis and also on a single accounting basis. So, you must operate hard to render your members significant and to keep them from canceling their membership subscription.

2. If your website offers some kind of information, content, or other tools for subscribers, you will constantly need to add fresh material to maintain your members there. You may need some kind of information or content. Members will always be prepared to withdraw their subscription if they sign up and then realize that you will never update or provide fresh subscription-only material. You must improve retention rates and maintain participants as soon as necessary in order to be efficient with your subscription web site. That implies that you always have to make sure that the content remains of relevance to your clients if you want to continue making money. Some individuals can look at the recurrent income from a subscription website and see it as a kind of passive income, which will continue to give you cash with very little input. On the contrary, this is a very time-consuming way of making cash, but this does not imply that time is not worth it. An exception is if you have a certain type of content-eating class so that participants can only access certain content depending on how soon they are a member. In order for participants to register

for a one-year course and then access a fresh module or class section on a monthly basis, for instance, you may be ready for a 12-part course. If you want access to all the contents you need, hold your subscription open throughout the year. You can do all in advance with this type of set-up and produce passive income, but once the one-year period has been completed your subscriber has no reason to maintain his / her subscription effective without any other advantage for members.

3. I had a fresh blog with a big public that I used as a forum to get fresh registrations when I began my subscription page. The development I discovered in the first year was even slower than I expected with that benefit. Many other subscription site holders I talked about over several years earlier had a comparable experience when it was harder than anticipated to establish a selling salary base. This is because I am pointing out that nobody stops beginning a registry gateway. I would like you to operate mentally and have some patience for it to operate. You will be much more likely to succeed in the long run if you have realistic expectations and are ready to keep working, even if you do not see a ton of growth.

4. The frequency of failed recurring payments is one of the greatest disadvantages of membership websites. PayPal does not give you much of an idea about why the transaction has failed, but it may include outdated credit card data of a customer (for example, the expiry date), insufficient customer account balances

or a lack of balance in the PayPal account. PayPal is not a good example. I do not have access to statistics anymore because I have been selling the database, but I believe that I have discovered about 25 percent of the recurring deals that have failed for some reason, excluding transfers that clients had refused prior to renewal. The end outcome for me was that I did not give monthly membership since I did not pay the tiny sum per month for the quantity of time it lasted to monitor the information. It was a mistake that a customer registered for one month's affiliation and did not make a second or third deposit. So, I only offered longer membership criteria which meant that, when the customer signed up, I received at least one bigger deposit. I could have prevented some of my issues by providing a different payment choice other than PayPal. I believe credit cards would have been slightly more precise in fewer successful operations, so I would suggest that you do not rely only on PayPal to charge membership fees.

5. You should expect it to take a ton of your time if you intend to handle everything linked to your membership website. Every location will, of course, vary, but it will be a lot of work to manage yourself a subscription website. By outsourcing some of the work, you can balance this. You can use someone to manage customer service, create content or personnel resources, manage your marketing and social media, or just about any other part of the operation of the site.

Chapter 6: Forex Trading

Foreign exchange is purchasing one currency and selling another currency at the same time. Currencies are traded in currency pairs through a broker or dealer, such as GBP / JPY or EUR / USD. This is the world's biggest financial market with a weekly amount exceeding $2 trillion US dollars. This exceeds three times the merged complete stock and futures exchanges.

The Forex spot market operates through bank networks, companies, and traders who exchange one currency for another. The absence of a tangible exchange but instead an electronic network allows the market to be operational 24 hours a day, spreading across main financial centers from one time zone to another. It is essential to keep in mind the crucial element of the absence of central exchange because it permeates every feature of the foreign exchange practice.

What Are Spot Markets?

This is any market that transacts with a monetary instrument's present value. Futures markets, like the Chicago Trade Board, give commodity bonds that have a shipping date that extends for several months into the future.

Foreign exchange spot transaction settlement generally takes place within two company days. Forex also has futures and forwards, but a large number of traders are using the spot market. We are discussing possibilities on the International Monetary Market to trade Forex futures.

Frequently Traded Currencies

The bigger brokers can trade any currency supported by a current country. The trading quantity (along with their signs) of the main currencies is provided in descending order: the U.S. Dollar (USD), Euro Dollar (EUR), Japanese Yen (JPY), British Pound Sterling (GBP), Canadian Dollar (CAD), Swiss Franc (CHF), and Australian Dollar (AUD). Every other currency is referred to as a minor and exotic from lesser nations.

Forex currency symbols are always three digits, with the first two digits identifying the country's name and the fifth letter identifying the currency's name. (The Swiss Franc abbreviation "CH" refers to Confederation Helvetica.) There is always a Forex exchange amid any two currencies. This often brings about some level of confusion among new traders who are inexperienced in trading in multi-currency markets (those who are primarily used to trading in either stock or futures markets where every trade is dominated by the dollar). A pair's cost is the ratio of their particular values.

Forex Traders

Trading currencies are categorized into two major groups. A smaller fraction of the daily foreign currency volume comes from businesses and governments that import or export commodities, and consequently have to transform these earnings into their own national currency, from the foreign currency earned during the business. Most now are stakeholders transacting for gain or speculation. Speculators vary from big companies trading a million or more currency units and maybe 1,000 or fewer units trading by the home-based provider. Retail Forex, just as it has grown over the past decade, still it is a very small representation of the total volume traded on a daily basis, but it is growing rapidly in numbers and significance.

Today, importers and exporters, worldwide portfolio managers, multinationals, high-frequency traders, speculators, day traders, long-term owners, and hedge funds all use the Forex sector to pay for products and facilities, to trade in financial assets, or to reduce the risk of currency movements by hedging their existence in other sectors.

British Pound (GBP) is an intrinsically lengthy British widget maker. If they enter into a long-term selling contract with a U.S. company, they may want to buy some U.S. dollar quantity and sell the same volume of the Great Britain Pound to hedge their earnings from a GBP fall.

By purchasing one currency while selling another currency at the same moment, the speculator trades to generate a profit. The hedger trades on a worldwide exchange to protect its margin (for example) against adverse currency modifications.

On one hand of the economy or the other, the hedger has an inherent stake. It's not the speculator. Speculation is not the wrong term. Speculators bring liquidity to a sector by setting efficient prices to make it simpler for everyone to transact the company. They also absorb marketplace hazards. This latter is different from the gambler who generates hazards for taking them.

Determining Currency Price

The determination of a currency price is dependent on a huge matrix of factors and conditions that are constantly changing, including political and economic stability. Other factors include interest rates, world trade, inflation, and deflation rates. In some instances, governments truly take part in the foreign currency exchange industry and usually have an effect on their currency's value.

Governments do this by mixing their national currency with the economy in an attempt to cut costs or, similarly, purchase to boost costs. The central bank considers this technique to be interference. Any of these factors can lead to elevated currency volatility, as well as large-scale company orders. The occurrence of abrupt changes in factors like the rate of employment can push the price of a currency considerably higher or decrease over a brief span of a moment. Technical factors can also influence currency prices for brief sentences, such as a well-known graph model.

However, it is hard for any organization to monitor the industry during a significant time because of the size and amount of the Forex market. The equation of the cost of a currency compared to another product is also shown by mob psychology and expectations. These variables have many correlations and are almost certainly not linear in nature. That implies that sometimes in an unpredictive manner, they constantly change and rearrange themselves. You don't see it now. The others can alter unnoticed if you concentrate on one or some of them. The concept of quantity recalls.

Forex Trading Costs

For as little as $1 can be initiated an online trading account for currency (a micro account). Getting a mini account costs anything from around $400. Don't laugh because these accounts are a wonderful way to get wet without soaking your feet. Unlike futures, you pick in Forex how much of any currency you want to purchase or sell, where the transfers set the volume of an agreement. Consequently, a grubstake of $4,000 is not appropriate as quickly as the trader takes part in incorrectly priced trades. Furthermore, Forex mini-accounts do not resist the non-liquid nature of many futures mini-contracts, as most of them buy from the same interbank monetary "pool." By demonstrating the allocation of the bid-ask, market makers carry their expenses and profit. ECN brokers charge a set lot price for the trade.

Comparison of Forex and Stocks

Historically, securities markets have been considered, at least by the bulk of the public, as an investment vehicle. In the past 10 years, securities have assumed a more speculative personality. This may have been due to the fall of the general stock market, as many security issues experienced unnecessary volatility due to the "unreasonable exuberance" displayed on the industry. The implied yield of an investment has no longer be applicable. Many traders engaged in day trading in the early 1990s rush only to discover that trading from a strategic point of perspective involves quite a bunch of cash, and the return—through, it is possible that it is higher than a long-term investment—was, to say the least, not linear.

After the day trader rush begins, many traders venture into the future stock index markets where they discovered they have better leverage on their property and not tie up their funds when they could receive interest or create cash elsewhere. Spot monetary trading, like futures exchanges, is an exceptional tool for model day traders who want to exploit their current wealth to trade. Spot currency trading offers traders with more options and impulsiveness while at the same time than the ones that are currently accessible inventory futures indexes. On the Forex market, former day securities traders have an excellent position

Forex and Futures Comparison

That, exactly, is the future contract— a lawful agreement to deliver or recognize the delivery in a distant future month of a particular grade and amount of a specific product. However, Forex is a business place (money) that barely reaches two business days. After two days, many Forex brokers enable their customers to keep trades open. Forex future or future agreements are in place, but spot market rollouts support most businesses.

In comparison with the above advantages, Forex transactions are practically always done at the time and price of the speculator. The ending of prospective traders after the clearing of the liquidation order has been uncovered in countless horrors. The elevated liquidity on the currency market (around three times as much as the complete amount of all future markets) ensures the quick and timely execution of all the orders (admission, rejection, and limitation, etc.)

The warning is something I'm talking about here in a subsequent section called a request or interference from the retailer.

The CFTC allows future dealers to establish regular boundaries on agreements which substantially hinder the ability to join or leave the industry at a chosen cost and moment. Such constraints do not apply in the Forex industry.

In terms of the United States, stock and futures traders are used to thinking dollar versus anything else, such as stock price or grain costs. Apples are comparable with oranges. But it's always a relationship in financial trade between one country and another–the fruit of someone is to animals of someone else. This paradigm shift may take a little while, but I will give you a whole host of examples to assist in building a fluid transition.

The author has been a trader and a trading advisor for merchandise for many years, but for many of the above-mentioned reasons, he found monetary trading in his interest.

I must reiterate: there is always a danger of speculation which is not subject to trading, regulation, or non-regulation of financial instruments. Leverage is a gate that moves in both directions.

Specific investment vehicles are denominated in USD or local currencies in inventories and futures traders need to create a similar transition to monetary trading. The Forex key car is a couple–the value of the contrast between currency and currency.

Advantages and Disadvantages of Forex Trading

Advantages of Forex Trading

No Commissions Charged

When trading with a market maker, certain fees such as clearing fees, exchange fees, public fees, brokerage fees, are not incurred.

No Brokers or Middle Men

Spot currency trading eliminates intermediaries and gives clients a chance to interact with market makers who are accountable for deciding on a particular currency pair when trading with an Electronic Communications Network (ECN) instantly.

Flexible Lot Size

The operations in the futures markets determine lots of contract sizes. A standard lot size arrangement for silver futures is 5,000 ounces. Even a silver "mini-contract" worth approximately $17,000, 1,000 ounces. In position FOREX, you have the chance to decide for yourself the optimal lot size for you. This makes it possible for traders to engage with accounts well below $1,000 efficiently. It also provides a significant cash management tool for astute traders.

Minimum Transactional Expenses

Transaction costs (the bid/ask spread) are usually below 0.1 percent in normal business conditions. The allocation at bigger distributors can go to as low as 0.07 percent. Currency prices are cited in pips.

High Liquidity

FOREX is the most fluid industry in the world with an average trading quantity of over $4 trillion a day. It means that it is absolutely possible for a company to enter and leave the sector at will, and in the short time frame, they may have lost or gained millions in profits.

Transactions Are Nearly Instantaneous

This is a beneficial by-product of elevated liquidity.

High Leverage, Small Margin

These factors enhance, and the opportunities for higher income (and losses) are consequently debated on. A 50% to 100% leverage is the most common, but traders have the flexibility of accessing up to 400$ leverage.

24-hour Market

Traders can take advantage of the market conditions at any time of the day in order to make a profit. The Forex market never has a bell which indicated the beginning or end of trading time.

Markets are shut from Friday night to Sunday afternoon. Usually, they go quiet at 5 p.m. As the economies move to the Asian Session. Around 7 p.m. The East's Standard Time.

Unrelated to the Stock Market

FOREX market trading means the sale or buys against another of one currency. There is, therefore, no hard correlation of the foreign-currency market with the stock market, although both are economic activity measures in some ways and can for a limited time be correlated in particular. Despite its comparative utility against other currencies, a bull market or a bear market for a currency is described. If we get a good perspective, we have a bull market in which we purchase the currency. Instead, we have a bull market for other currencies, if the perspective is pessimistic, and traders make incomes by replacing the currency with other currencies. There is always a good trading chance for a trader in either situation. Even if there are often large cost changes, the chance of a monetary collapse is lower than stocks because the comparative importance is evaluated by a couple. The United States currency (USD) may be deep-rooted, but the Euro (EUR) may be so. The play is the two-way ratio. The U.S. is the top four traded currencies. USD (USD), EUR, JPY, and GBP (GBP). Dollar (USD). Fund managers are becoming interested in FOREX due to this lack of correlation with other investments.

Interbank Market

FOREX has a network of global distributors at its heart. They are primarily large companies that interact and trade via electronic networks and telephone with each other and their customers. No organized exchanges can act as the main location to create serving equity markets simpler on the New York Stock Exchange. The FOREX market works in a way comparable to the US NASDAQ industry and is also known as the OTC industry. All aspects of currency trading are affected by the absence of a centralized exchange.

The Market Can't Be Cornered

The FOREX market is so vast and has so many people who cannot be regulated for an extended duration by any single organization and not even a central bank. Even powerful central bank actions are progressively failing and becoming short-lived. As a result, central banks are becoming less and less susceptible to market price manipulation. (There is no reason to note that efforts have been made at the end of the 1970s in order to decrease the silver exchange industry. Such a disruptive excess is unlikely to happen during Forex exchange activities.) Fraud opportunities are considerably less than in any other funding tool, at least against the scheme itself as a whole.

Regulation Is Limited

Regulation limits the legislative impact on Forex transactions, mainly because no centralized location or exchange exists. However, most nations have a say in the law, and there are other things going on. However, fraud is always fraud in any country and is punished by criminal penalties. There are now certain restricted Forex retail supervisory units such as the Commodity Futures Trading Commission (CFTC) and the NFA.

Trading Is Done Online

The ability to trade over the internet has been an incentive for FOREX retail. You can pick from over 100 online broker-dealers for FOREX today. The trader has at his disposal a wide variety of alternatives, given the fact that none is ideal.

Third-party Products and Services

Retail Forex's enormous popularity has fostered a thriving third-party products and services sector.

Disadvantages of Forex Trading

Counterparty Risks

The Forex market is a global industry. Consequently, Forex market regulation is a challenging problem because it concerns the sovereignty of many nations ' currencies. This generates a situation that mainly unregulated the Forex market. There is, therefore, no centralized exchange that ensures risk-free trade execution. Consequently, when buyers or traders enter into trades, they must also be aware of the default risk they face, i.e., the danger that the counterparty may not have the desire or capacity to fulfill the agreements. Therefore, Forex trading includes a thorough evaluation of counterparty hazards and the development of schemes to mitigate them.

Process of Price Determination

FOREX is often believed to have a complex method of determining prices because the process is a composite price determination. Exchange rates are determined by quite a number of variables and reasons. International politics and the economy usually affect the rate of the currency, and this causes it to have a great level of uncertainty. Forex trading is usually conducted on a technical analysis basis and indicators, which in most cases are usually inadequate to define this kind of variation.

Leverage Risks

The highest leverage is provided by Forex exchanges. The term leverage automatically involves danger, and a 20 to 30-fold gearing ratio involves a ton of danger! Since there are no limits to the amount of movement that could occur in a given day on the Forex market, a person may lose all of their investment in a matter of minutes if they place highly leveraged bets. Novice investors are more likely to make such mistakes because they don't know how much danger it carries with it!

Operational Risks

Forex trading activities are hard to operate. This is because the Forex market is functioning all the moment while people are not! Hence, when they are away, traders must resort to algorithms to safeguard the importance of their assets. Alternatively, multinational companies are spreading trading desks around the globe. This can only be achieved, however, if trading takes place on a very big scale. Therefore, if a person doesn't have the assets or understand how to handle their jobs when they're away, Forex prices could trigger important night or weekend value loss.

Minimal Transparency

This is one of the foreign exchange market's greatest disadvantages. Due to the nature of the foreign exchange market's being decentralized and de-regularized, it is dominated by brokers. And you've got to trade with experts. Being a broker-driven means not being fully transparent on the Forex market. A trader may have no power over how his trading order will be performed, but you may not get the highest cost, or you may have restricted opinions on trading returns as provided by your broker. Therefore, an easy recommendation is to cope only with controlled brokers that fall within the competence of well-reputed banks. Regulators are not controlling the industry, but they can regulate broker operations.

Lack of a Central Exchange

The spot Forex market has no centralized swap or clearinghouse, unlike stocks or futures. Alternatively, each broker functions as their own exchange, and the broker becomes the market maker efficiently. This, in reality, gives the broker a chance to abuse it or worse. We also see cost differences from broker to broker due to the lack of a centralized return.

These distinctions will be low when interacting with reputable brokers in well-regulated nations, but you need to be well conscious of this, particularly if your mapping information supplier is not the same as your broker, as this may result in inconsistencies between the scheduled and real execution of trades.

Highly Volatile

Forex trading has a degree of volatility which, by contrast, makes the most effective stock market seem fluid. Market forces, central bank policies, and economic disasters can trigger enormous currency market shifts. As of the release date, almost $4 trillion trades hands every day in Forex exchanges, so a tiny ripple in one or more currencies can trigger a tidal wave of purchasing and selling. Investor accounts in Forex economies that are over-leveraged or under-educated may bring catastrophic hits.

Improper Learning Curve

While there is a benefit that loads of teaching instruments and equipment are accessible at no cost, there is also a danger involved. In the stock market, portfolio executives, trade consultants, and relationship executives can provide skilled help to a trader. Contrary to that, with little or no help, Forex traders must trade on their own. Therefore, disciplined and continuous self-directed teaching throughout the trading profession is crucial. Most beginners effectively leave during the original phase, primarily owing to losses owing to a restricted understanding of Forex trading and inappropriate trading.

A Non-Stop Market

There are no closing bells or holiday breaks on Forex exchanges. Traders must be ready for a market that takes place 24/7/365. Forex traders on one hand of the world can create profits while sleeping as traders on the other hand of the globe try to enhance their roles. A mentally exhausting practice can be an effort to follow the steady changes in exchange rates, coupled with the volatile nature of currency trading.

Chapter 7: Efficient Business Operations

When Michael Dell was growing his company rapidly, he reached a point in the mid-'90s when he ran out of cash. He was "growing broke," like so many other businesses scaling up quickly. That's when he brought in Tom Meredith as CFO. Meredith calculated Dell Inc.'s cash conversion cycle (CCC) to be 63 days. That meant it took 63 days from the time Dell spent a dollar on anything until it flowed back through the business and onto the balance sheet (into the bank) as cash.

Focusing on one cash improvement strategy/initiative every 90 days, Meredith drove the CCC to negative 21 days by the time he left Dell a decade later. This meant the company received a dollar 21 days before it had to be spent on anything. As Dell grew faster, it generated cash instead of consuming it. That is why the founder and CEO had sufficient cash to contribute to taking the company private in 2013. In this chapter, we'll examine strategies for accelerating your cash flow through improvements in your CCC.

Cash Conversion Cycle (CCC)

Not every business can have a negative CCC, but you can view Dell's example as inspiration to move yours in that direction. It is just a matter of looking for ways to improve it. For instance,

Catapult Systems LLC, an Austin-based, Microsoft-focused IT consulting company, used to bill clients on a 30-day cycle. Meanwhile, employees were paid twice a month, leading to what founder and Chairman Sam Goodner call "a terrible cash-flow story." He simply started billing his clients twice per month after finding more than 90% were agreeable to the change. This nearly doubled cash flow immediately. To tackle the cash conversion cycle, start by reading "How Fast Can Your Company Afford to Grow?" It provides the formulas to help your team calculate the company's overall CCC and discusses many of the financial levers highlighted in the last chapter of this "Cash" section of the book.

Cash Acceleration Strategies (CASh)

To help teams brainstorm ways to improve their cash conversion cycles, we created a one-page tool called Cash Acceleration Strategies, or CASh. It breaks down the CCC into four main components:

Most businesses will have some aspect of each of these cash cycle components. Even service firms have a form of inventory if they have underutilized their staff. What might differ is the sequence of these components, with some cycles overlapping others or occurring in a different order? For instance, if the structure of your business model is to collect the payment in advance, like Dell, then the billing and payment cycle occurs after the selling cycle but before the production and delivery cycle. (In other words, Dell arranged to take ownership of inventory only after a computer was sold.)

We encourage management teams to set aside an hour or more each month to brainstorm ways to improve each of these cash cycle components. This is a powerful exercise to do with the broader middle-management team at half-day to the full-day monthly management meeting. It will give everyone a better understanding of how cash flows through the business and how each function can contribute positively.

Some areas of opportunity include:

> First, avoid saying, "Well, that's just how it's in our industry."
> Ensure that your easy money recorded DAILY, with a brief description of why it has changed over the past 24 hours and graph it against daily accounts receivable (AR) and accounts payable (AP). When you see how the money flows on a regular basis, you will know so much more about your company.
> If you want earlier payment, request. Small firms find that big firms (and governments!!) are going to pay much quicker or even prepaid if they just ask.
> Return value to clients who pay in advance or on purchase.
> Get your invoices out faster. Hire another billing individual to do nothing but ensure prompt invoicing and payment follow-up.

- Send friendly reminders that payments are due five days before the deadline. Many clients are disorganized, and the reminders will be appreciated, leading to faster payment.
- If invoices are recurring, receive your clients' recurrent loan card permission to automate on-time transactions.
- Comprehend why your customers pay late. With your item or service, they may be dissatisfied. Or maybe an invoice has recurring errors or is not organized to pass through the automated invoicing scheme of the customer.
- Understand the payment schedules of each customer, and moment to match with your deposits.
- Pay a credit card for a lot of your own costs so you can play the float.
- Get your own clients to pay by credit card, so even if their cash flow is slow, they can reward you rapidly.
- Help your clients enhance their cash flow to enable them to reward you at the moment. For example, offer them rental alternatives.
- Shorten your item or service delivery cycles. You all have some sort of "progressive job." The quicker you full tasks, the quicker you get compensated.
- Offer a precious item or service that gives your clients some leverage to get them to pay earlier.
- Remember, money is enhanced by enhancing profits and profit.

Almost all of these ideas fall into three general categories where you can make improvements:

1. Cut cycle times.
2. Remove mistakes.
3. Modify the business model.

To further stimulate your thinking, here are some ideas in each category that can help you improve cash flow.

Cut Cycle Times

Increasing the pace of everything your company does (e.g., decreasing the time it takes to complete a full cycle from customer interest to completed transaction) helps your CCC. This is why we are fans of applying Toyota's Lean process to all aspects of the business. With its focus on eliminating wasted time, it's an ideal tool to improve processes, increase employee productivity, and accelerate cash flow.

Pay particular attention to the sales process. You may be spending enormous amounts of money and time on landing customers. Using negotiation techniques taught by Victoria Medvec (check out her powerful online "High Stakes Negotiation" course at *scalingup.com*), firms like Goldman Sachs have reduced sales cycles from months to weeks and from weeks to days. The quicker you can get a deal in the door, the quicker the cash starts flowing — and you thwart would-be competitors.

On the production side, back when Dell had factories, a production worker could assemble a computer in minutes, and the company held only a few days' worth of inventory. This rapid turn of inventory and the speed of manufacturing contributed hugely to the impressive CCC the company achieved. Because many accounting departments are short-handed, there are often delays in getting invoices sent out and bills collected. Besides billing twice per month to improve cash flow, Catapult Systems collects faster than most firms. Notes Goodner, the chairman: "Our collections person in the accounting department works hard to create a personal rapport with our clients' accounts payable teams. She is the most charming, disarming, non-threatening, likable person you could possibly have. She starts calling the accounting departments of our clients five days before the check is due just to make sure everything is okay and says that we are doing great on the project. She gives her number just in case anything comes up and says, 'I really look forward to getting that check from you next week.'" And if the check is late, the Catapult Systems' collections specialist places a call to the client the next day. That is another reason to bolster your accounting department resources.

Goodner credits this approach with his company's "unbelievably high" track record of getting paid on time — simply because, he says, "We ask for it." Meanwhile, a firm in Australia sends inexpensive lottery tickets as thank-you to its customers' accounts payable clerks when they pay invoices on time. When customers are faced with a stack of bills to pay, this company's invoices seem to make it to the top of the pile magically! And if this might be frowned upon (or deemed illegal) in your industry or locale, a holiday card showing appreciation to the people in accounts payable can achieve the same effect. The point is to have someone pay attention to the accounts payable people!

Also specify a due date (May 31, for example) on the invoice rather than include the standard "due in 30 days." Often, someone higher up in the client organization has to sign off on an invoice before it can be paid, with the 30-day clock starting when this signature is received. If there is a specific due date, even if the signature isn't obtained until the day before, the payables clerk will assume that the sign-off authorizes the payment to occur on the date specified and will pay the bill immediately. Examine all of the processes in the organization — sales, production, service delivery, billing, and collections — and find ways to speed up and move cash more quickly through the business.

Remove Mistakes

Nothing infuriates customers more than a mistake. It is the #1 reason they are slow to pay. And incomplete orders, invoicing errors, and missed deadlines are not only costly but also drag down the very processes you want to speed up, snarling cash flow. Adam Sproule, founder of Salisbury Landscaping in Alberta, has the company's cash conversion cycle down to a fine art. The approach he has used has helped him optimize the CCC for the past 20 years. Besides securing deposits upfront (with the final payment due immediately upon a project's completion), Salisbury Landscaping has put operating practices in place to finish jobs quickly and in a far less disruptive way than clients usually see in its industry. This, in turn, has given Salisbury a reputation that makes collecting deposits and payments easier.

Tradespeople in landscaping or construction usually work on two to three jobs at the same time, often leaving customers wondering what's happening and why the projects aren't finished yet. "It's a real pet peeve of people we talk to," says Sproule. Instead, Salisbury's crews focus on one job at a time, getting in and out as quickly as possible. "We deal with live plants, so we want to finish quickly," Sproule says. "Not only is it a major disruption to our clients if we don't, but the longer we take, the more likely there will be problems." As soon as the crew leaves, a member of Sproule's team walks around with the customer to make sure the job is absolutely perfect. "Even if there are just a couple deficiencies, we write them down," says Sproule, who notes that his staff refers to corrections of deficiencies as "adjustments," to avoid any negative perception. "We then make an adjustment list. Because we're very efficient at what we do, the customer has no reason to doubt us. So, a lot of times, they give us the full payment immediately after the walk-around even if there are a few things left to do," notes Sproule. And to close the loop of learning and avoid making the same mistakes on subsequent projects,

Salisbury sends out the same crew that generated the deficiencies to handle the adjustments quickly.

PPR Talent Management Group freed up a million dollars every month through improved accuracy in its invoicing. Serving the needs of a thousand clients — mostly hospitals, all with different policies and time-sheet protocols — caused considerable complexity in invoicing. As a result, clients delayed paying while PPR sorted out the errors on its invoices. To address this issue, the Florida company hired an additional person not only to build relationships with the payables departments but also to customize invoices to match each specific hospital's billing codes. As CEO Dwight Cooper notes, "When we changed our process and got it right, the confidence level with our clients came up fast." Then the latest recession came. As it dragged on into 2009, Cooper says, "We took our eye off the cash ball." It was time to change the entire business model — at least from a cash perspective.

Change the Business Model

For PPR, collections were not the problem; it was creating the right terms, to begin with. To grow the business, PPR needed cash, so it asked customers to pay in advance. "We were pleasantly surprised when many of our customers just said yes," says Cooper. There are many adjustments you can make to your business model that positively affect your CCC. The two with the biggest results are getting your customers to fund your business, much like Costco does via membership fees, or having suppliers do this, as Dell did through its inventory management. For sources of cash other than loans or investors, we refer you to a *Fortune* Small Business article Verne wrote titled "Finding Money You Didn't Know You Had": *http://tiny.cc/finding-money*

Improving Profitability

Benetton India also felt the crunch of the economic downturn in 2009, so it embarked on a major cost-saving initiative. Sanjeev Mohanty, CEO of Benetton India Private Ltd., got vendors to bid online for contracts using business commerce software purchased from Ariba. "Initially, everyone was very skeptical, saying that we would lose quality," he says. Plus, some suppliers had been providing goods to Benetton India for more than a decade, and executives hesitated to disrupt what appeared to be working well.

Mohanty persisted, and the savings have been significant. For instance, Benetton India invited six different suppliers, including the incumbent, to bid on its contract for shopping bags. Suppliers can use Ariba not only to place their bids, but also to see what other companies are bidding. Normally, the whole bidding process can take several hours, but this round closed in 32 minutes, while the executive team watched in real-time. Benetton previously paid 52 cents per shopping bag, and the final bid came in at 34 cents —huge savings.

Surprisingly, the incumbent supplier provided the final low bid, so in addition to benefiting from the savings, Benetton India maintained the same-quality bag. Today, company employees must use Ariba to procure any goods or services with a value of more than $10,000. In one recent year, Benetton India saved $1.2 million through this procurement process.

Again, when you improve profitability, it improves cash — as long as you're not funding management waste on the balance sheet, as we'll discuss further in the next two chapters. And for retail companies like MOM's Organic Market and Benetton India, which collect cash or credit card payments for every transaction, the only real internal financial cash lever is on the P&L side of the business.

During the recent financial crisis, fearing credit lines might dry up, MOM's CEO Scott Nash and his team stayed laser-focused on improving profitability (emphasizing pricing, purchasing, etc.). Today, with four times industry average profitability, the metro Washington-based chain has driven up its free operating cash flow to fund its continued expansion.

Completing Your Cash Acceleration Strategies (CASh) Tool

1. Read the article titled "How Fast Can Your Company Afford to Grow?" It is a Harvard business review.
2. Calculate your existing CCC in days.
3. Calculate the amount of cash required to fund each additional day of CCC.
4. Brainstorm ways to improve your CCC and the seven financial levers highlighted in the last chapter of this "Cash" section using the one-page CASh tool. Be sure to explore ways in all three general categories — shortening cycle times, eliminating mistakes, and changing the business model — for each segment of the CCC.
5. Choose one cash-improvement initiative every 90 days as one of your quarterly priorities (Rocks). Imagine you improve your CCC by 30 days (and you run a $30 million business). You now have $2.5 million extra in your bank account, and you can:
   a) Pay down your operating credit line.
   b) Distribute a dividend to shareholders.
   c) Invest in a new project that will support your growth plans.
   d) Sit on it until you find the perfect opportunity.
   e) Keep it as insurance for when times get rough.

The best part about improving your CCC is that it usually results in your business pulsing faster, which is better for the customer.

It will also improve the business savvy of your managers as they become more aware of the impact of their decisions on cash flow. And with more cash in the bank, everyone will sleep better as you scale up the business. This is one routine that will really set you free and give you sticking power in the market.

Business Startup Costs

Business Type	Description	Cost Estimation
Affiliate Marketing	Domain name	From $10 per annum
	Website Logo	From $10
	Website Design plus Hosting from wix.com	From $4.50 per month
Creating Online Courses	iSpring Suite	$970 Annually
Social Media influencing	For positive and lasting results, use your social skills.	$0
Membership Websites	Finepoint.com	$450 - $1200 Annually
Forex Trading	Depends on the amount of capital you are willing to spend	From $10

Conclusion

To close out this topic, I want to leave you with some encouragement. Creating passive revenue streams takes time, effort, and the willingness to stretch outside of your comfort zone. You may not feel comfortable doing a teleseminar or putting your thoughts out there in a book, but I can assure you that once you do it, you won't go back to solely trading time for money. Something we did not discuss at length but is vitally important is the idea of perfectionism.

Creating products should be a fun and flexible journey for you. Know that it is better to get a product out and tweak/edit it later than it is for it to never make it to your audience. You can always change and modify a product or issue a version 2.0 of a program, but you won't have the opportunity if it doesn't exist. When it comes to creating passive revenue streams, be fearless. The benefit will far outweigh the risk in 99.9% of scenarios. It is my greatest hope that this book has provided you with enough material to make great strides in the creation of multiple streams of income.

You can combine one or more of the ideas shared in this book to generate some quality passive income. As we have seen, if these ideas do not work for you, just feel free to get the message put forth and incorporate them into your own ideas to ensure your venture is a success.

Made in the USA
Monee, IL
31 December 2019